ADMIRALS OF THE CARIBBEAN

SIR FRANCIS DRAKE

ADMIRALS
OF THE CARIBBEAN

BY

FRANCIS RUSSELL HART

WITH ILLUSTRATIONS

 BOOKS FOR LIBRARIES PRESS
FREEPORT, NEW YORK

First Published 1922
Reprinted 1971

F
2161
H35
1971

INTERNATIONAL STANDARD BOOK NUMBER:
0-8369-5949-3

LIBRARY OF CONGRESS CATALOG CARD NUMBER:
77-165640

PRINTED IN THE UNITED STATES OF AMERICA

PREFACE

THE romantic interest which attaches to the wa/ ters of the Caribbean has to some extent obscured the fact that the records of events in the Caribbean during the sixteenth, seventeenth, and eighteenth centuries are an integral part of the history of England and of the American colonies. Battles fought in the Caribbean Sea were often an important factor in making peace or war in Europe.

Not only were settlements established in the West Indies and in the Spanish Main a century in advance of those in North America, but for three hundred years the struggles of the European nations for the control of the commerce of this region had a direct effect upon the material, political, and racial development of the North American colonies.

During the last quarter of the sixteenth century, Spain was the strongest of European powers. In the New World, Spanish rule was practically absolute from Labrador to the Rio de la Plata on the Atlantic side and from the Isthmus south on the western coast of South America; in fact a Papal grant had divided the American continent between Portugal and Spain. The arrogant claim of the Spanish Crown was contested only by a small French set/

tlement on the St. Lawrence and in Labrador by Fro⁄
bisher's Adventure. The story of the great seamen of
Elizabeth's reign — Drake, Hawkins, and Frobisher —
is almost the history of the England of their day; the
battles they fought made the settlements in Virginia and
Massachusetts possible.

Of no less influence in the development of the English
colonial settlements were the naval undertakings of Sir
Henry Morgan in the seventeenth, and of Admiral Ver⁄
non and Admiral Rodney in the eighteenth, century.

It was the final supremacy of British control of the
Caribbean Sea which made the Rio Grande the northern
boundary of Latin⁄America instead of the Potomac.

The monographs which have been here brought to⁄
gether were written as a contribution to the better under⁄
standing of West Indian history; those on Drake and on
the French Expedition to Cartagena were printed some
years ago in an historical publication in America; that
on Vernon appeared in "Hispania" (London) and in
Spanish in the Boletin de Historia y Antiqüedades de la
Academia Nacional de Historia (Bogotá).

All of these have been made the subject of revision
and extension. The accounts of Morgan and Rodney have
not been previously published.

Boston, 1922

CONTENTS

ILLUSTRATIONS

The fold-out map is from an old French map engraved by H. van Loon
and published in Paris in 1705

ADMIRALS OF THE CARIBBEAN

ADMIRALS OF THE CARIBBEAN

CHAPTER 1

THE EARLY NAVIGATORS

THE voyager approaching the Caribbean Sea to-day from the north passes through the same gateway and makes the same first landfall as did Columbus on his first voyage. At sunrise on the 13th October, 1492, the first of the great Caribbean Admirals, Christopher Columbus, landed on a small island which he named San Salvador. A comparison of the data contained in his records with the actual description and locations of the small islands which form the northern Bahamas makes it practically certain that the island at the northern entrance to the Crooked Island passage which bears the name of San Salvador* is the actual first landing-place of Columbus in the New World.

This New World, it is to be remembered, Columbus did not himself then recognize as such, but believed he had reached the outposts of the Indies, and that the innumerable small islands which he found were those described by Marco Polo. For this reason Columbus gave to the lands which he had discovered the name "West Indies,"

---

* The native name of this island was Guanahani ; on many charts it is marked Watling's Island.

and the mild but somewhat frightened natives were called "Indians." It was at this first little island that a new commerce had its beginnings. Columbus in his diary describes the exchange of commodities with the natives as follows: "They afterwards came swimming to the ships' boats "where we were, and brought us parrots and balls of cotton thread and assegais and many other things, and exchanged them for various commodities such as little glass "beads and small bells." It was noticed that some of the natives wore small ornaments of gold; Columbus by signs enquired as to the origin of this gold and was told that it came from lands to the south. After stops at various other small islands, he reached one which appeared so large that he was uncertain as to whether it were island or continent. By the natives it was called Cuba.

The Spaniards were charmed with the beauty and fertility of the island. Gold ornaments were more plentiful than on the lesser islands and Columbus was assured that the gold came from the mountains of the interior. Not wholly satisfied with the amount of gold trinkets obtained in exchange for beads and the like, and the descriptions of the places from which it came being somewhat illusive, Columbus proceeded to Haiti where he was told gold was even more plentiful. Here gold in considerable quantities was found, but still it was to the distant mountains that the natives pointed as the inexhaustible source. The belief that he was on the borders of Marco Polo's Cathay and

Cipango was so fixed in the mind of Columbus that knowledge of the great reality of his accomplishment was long deferred. It was here on the island of Haiti, which the Spaniards named Hispaniola, that the first European settlement was attempted.

Thirtyeight of his company were left by Columbus to form the base for a colony. It was expected that, by the time Columbus should return with a larger expedition, those left behind would have learned somewhat of the language, explored the country, and discovered the gold mines.

In January, 1493, Columbus left the newly established settlement, taking with him a few of the natives and all the gold he had collected. With the events of the transAtlantic voyages of Columbus and his varied treatment at home we are not here concerned.

The accounts of the New World given by Columbus and his companions needed little exaggeration to incite the ambition and greed of Ferdinand. The second expedition was made up of seventeen ships carrying fifteen hundred persons and reached Hispaniola in November, 1493. Columbus found his settlement wholly destroyed and the few survivors of the original band scattered about the island.

The settlers left by Columbus had been without competent leadership and had through violence and cruelty inflamed the natives. In no way discouraged by the failure of his first attempt, Columbus selected a better site, planned and laid out an adequately protected city, which he named Isabella in honour of the Queen. This was the first endur' ing settlement founded by Europeans in the New World.

Even in these early days the fortunes of the Western Hemisphere were handicapped by the tangled diplomacy of the Old World. The Pope with prodigal hand had granted to Portugal all the countries that had been or might be discovered between Capes Nun and Bojador, on the African coast, to India. The lands discovered by Co' lumbus and appropriately claimed by Spain were, of course, within this territory covered by the over'generous blanket assignment to Portugal. It was Pope Martin V who had made the grant to Portugal. Spain as well as Portugal was devoutly Catholic, and although she may have had men' tal reservations as to the actual authority of the Pope to dispose of possible lands and continents, of the location of which he could have no exact knowledge or of the exist' ence of which he was in ignorance, she applied to the new Pope, Alexander VI, and obtained a specific grant of all the islands and mainland discovered or to be discovered by Spain in the Western Ocean. To reconcile the two Papal grants it was decreed that all territory east of a north'and' south line drawn one hundred miles west of the Azores should belong to Portugal and all territory west of the same line should belong to Spain. At a later period an excep' tion was made and Brazil was allotted to Portugal.

The authority of the Pope to dispose of the New World was based on the assumption that the care of the heathen had been placed by God in the hands of the Pope, who had, therefore, the right to select his agents to perform the holy duty.

On this second voyage of Columbus, after leaving his brother, Diego, as Governor of the new colony at Isabella in Hispaniola, Columbus discovered and coasted about the island of Jamaica. From Jamaica he returned to Isabella and found that the colonists, free from his authoritative control and in spite of his cautions, had again embroiled themselves with the natives. Under the direct guidance of the great Admiral, it is probable that mild measures would have sufficed to make the rule of the invaders supreme over the fairly docile Carib Indians; but Diego Columbus and the Military Commander, de Ojeda, were unequal to their tasks, and Columbus on his return resorted to brutal measures to subdue the island. One of the chief caciques was taken with other prisoners to the ships; a heavy tribute was imposed on all Indians over fourteen years of age. In the spring of 1496, Columbus returned to Spain, this time leaving his brother Bartolomé in charge of the colony.

It was in August, 1498, that his third voyage brought him again to the West Indies and his first landfall was a new island which he named and which is still called Trinidad. His discoveries brought him to the near-by mouth of the Orinoco River, the great size of which and its many mouths made him rightly conclude that he had at last reached a great continent.

Of all the great New World which Columbus by his knowledge, courage, and perseverance discovered, this territory, stretching from near the Orinoco to Panamá, was the only part which was to bear in part his name and be called Colombia.* So beautiful did the country appear to Columbus and his companions that it was believed to be the actual Terrestrial Paradise and the presumptive source of the Orinoco to be the Garden of Eden. Upon his arrival at Hispaniola he again found affairs in a bad state; his brother Bartolomé possessed prudence, but appeared to have lacked the forcefulness necessary to exact obedience from his associates. News of the disorder in the colony had reached Spain. The enemies of Columbus had found the ears of Ferdinand and Isabella. Rights and privileges which had been granted to Columbus as Viceroy were cancelled, and he went back to Spain a prisoner.

Undaunted by difficulties, he overcame all opposition and, following his original aim, he attempted by a fourth expedition to find a short route to India. At the advanced age of sixty-six, with his brother Bartolomé and his son Fernando, he sailed from Spain in 1502. On this voyage

* Three centuries later the wars of secession against Spain resulted in the separation of what is now Venezuela from Nueva Granada. The region to the West was named Colombia.

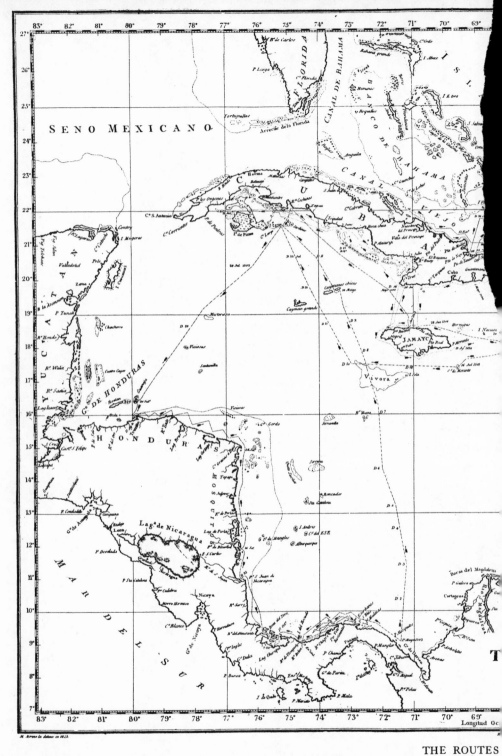

THE ROUTES

(From Coleccion de los Viages y Descubrimie

Num. 2.

Carta
de las Costas de
TIERRA FIRME
DESDE EL RIO ORINOCO HASTA YUCATAN
y de las islas Antillas y Lucayas
CON LAS DERROTAS QUE SIGUIO
Dⁿ Cristobal Colon
en sus descubrimientos por estos mares.

Viage Iº en 1492 y 93.
Viage IIº en 1493. 94. 95 y 96.
Viage IIIº en 1498.
Viage IVº en 1502. 3 y 4

OF COLUMBUS

os por Fernandez de Navarrete, Madrid, 1825)

he discovered Martinique and cruised along the whole coast of Central America from Cape Gracias á Dios to Porto Bello on the Isthmus of Panamá. Through the loss of two of his four ships he was forced to abandon his explorations, although still convinced that the Isthmus of Darien would prove to be a point around which would be found the route to India.

Five centuries later the construction of the Panama Canal made the dream of Columbus a reality.

On the way from Porto Bello to Hispaniola, Columbus was wrecked on the island of Jamaica, and it was not until 1504 that, greatly aged, ill and depressed in spirits, he again reached Spain. He died at Valladolid on the 12th of May, 1506. It was as a discoverer and not as a colonizer that Columbus left his impress upon the New World.

During the first century after their discovery, the West Indies were under the almost exclusive domination of Spain. The subsequent decadence of that great power has bred a misconception of her powerful and extraordinary initiative in connection with the settlement of the New World.

The later invasion of the Anglo-Saxon and the influence of theological bias has developed a tendency to exalt the exploits of those who followed the path which was first blazed by the *Conquistadores* and to underrate the courage and undaunted spirit shown in the Spanish adventures in the New World. It is not wholly true that

Spain the Conqueror was solely an avaricious oppressor of the peoples which she subdued. Nor is it true that the English adventurers who followed were actuated solely by religious aspirations. Yet those are the impressions to be gained from popular textbooks. It is true, however, that the same causes which have led to the modern de/ cadence of Spain made of her a bad colonizer, and that the spirit shown by even the early English navigators and ad/ venturers was more adapted to successfully effect perma/ nent occupation of the conquered lands. In the fifteenth and sixteenth centuries all nations which competed for a share in the rich booty of the Western World were im/ pelled by the same motives, and to none can be attributed a monopoly of either vice or virtue.

During the period in which the Spanish domination of the Caribbean was complete and for a considerable time unchallenged, great progress was made in exploration. Fortified towns were built and a system of government established. Assisted by the merchants of Seville, many of those who had accompanied Columbus on one or more of his voyages undertook on their own accounts further voyages of discovery and conquest. In 1499, Alonzo de Ojeda, who had accompanied Columbus on his second voyage, followed the track of the great discoverer to Terra Firma and continued the exploration to the Gulf of Paria and Cape Vela. The Florentine, Amerigo Vespucci, who later was to give his name to the two continents of Amer/

ica and who had been of the company of Columbus on one voyage, was a companion of de Ojeda.

At the same time Pedro Alonzo Niño, who had been with Columbus on his third voyage, conducted a success- ful trading venture, and Vicente Pinzon, who had been with Columbus on his first voyage, explored the coast of Brazil. In the meantime the Portuguese Vasco da Gama had rounded the Cape of Good Hope and opened the road to the East Indies. Diego Lepe doubled Cape St. Augustine and explored the coast beyond it to the southwest. In 1501, Rodrigo de Bastidas and Juan de la Cosa doubled Cape Vela and added some three hundred miles to the known coast-line. Their discoveries included the Gulf of Darien where a few years later the port of Nombre de Dios was established.

That this record of successful navigation and discovery was possible within so few years and with vessels of so small a size is a marvel, and that more were not lost is testi- mony to the high courage and expert seamanship of these early voyagers.

Tidings of the great West Indian adventure of Spain awoke in the other countries of Europe a spirit of emula- tion. Lethargic England as well as Portugal entered the race for a share in the wealth of the New World. The Cabots, Venetians who had settled at Bristol, explored from Labrador southward, but were obliged to return to Bristol before reaching the West Indies. At the end of the first decade of the sixteenth century, Juan Ponce de Leon had settled and established a firm government on the island of Puerto Rico, which had been discovered by Columbus on his second voyage. Juan Diaz de Solis and Vicente Pinzon explored Yucatan.

Up to 1509, the excitements of discovery and the rewards of casual looting had so occupied the explorers that no organized attempt had been made to establish settlements in a large way or to organize a comprehensive system of government. In 1509, de Ojeda, accompanied by Vasco Nuñez de Balboa, de la Cosa, and Pizarro—men destined to later play a great part in the development of regions outside of the Caribbean Sea — took part in an expedition to establish settlements on the mainland. Ferdinand granted titles and patents with a generous hand. Ojeda was made Governor of all the country between Cape Vela and the Gulf of Darien, and Diego de Nicuesa, who had gained wealth and experience in Hispaniola, was made Governor of the country between Darien and Cape Gracias á Dios. These two long stretches of coast became known as the Spanish Main.

In 1510, Diego Velazquez conquered the island of Cuba. Two years later, Ponce de Leon fitted out an expedition in Puerto Rico and explored Florida. The Gulf of Mexico was quite fully explored by de Piñeda. Vasco Nuñez de Balboa, who had accompanied de Ojeda, had been made Governor of a small settlement at Darien and

CUZCO, THE RICHEST CITY OF THE WHOLE PERUVIAN KINGDOM,
IS TAKEN BY THE SPANIARDS

(Theodore de Bry, 1596)

had heard stories of the great sea beyond the land. With a considerable company and great difficulty he crossed the isthmus and found a great ocean, of which he took possession in the name of the King of Spain. On account of the east-and-west direction of the two coasts of the isthmus, Balboa reached the Pacific by travelling southward, and not unnaturally named his discovery the South Sea. A few years later when Magellan reached the same ocean, he named it the Pacific.

In the company of Velazquez when he conquered Cuba had been Hernan Cortez who was destined to become perhaps the best known, both for his conquests and his cruelties, of any of the Spanish conquerors. In 1518, with a large expedition he began the subjugation of Mexico. It required nearly three years to completely overcome the powerful Montezuma.

About this period (1524), Francisco Pizarro began his exploration of the West Coast which finally resulted in the expedition which a few years later accomplished the conquest of the great empire of the Incas called Peru.

In the decade between 1530 and 1540, the work of conquest and occupation progressed without interruption. Nueva Granada, made up of what is now Colombia and Venezuela, were added to the Spanish dominions. The important cities of Cartagena and Santa Marta were founded and some semblance to an organized government maintained. Development or commerce in the proper meanings of the words did not, however, take place. Plundering of the conquered Indians was the only established business.

It is unfortunate that those responsible for the most important discoveries of the Christian era should have been guilty of atrocious and unnecessary cruelties. Even measured by the standards of the time, the treatment of the native peoples was inhuman and wanton in its barbarities. In many places the native population was almost annihilated.

Oviedo in describing the malignant cruelties practised by Governor Pediarias and his Lieutenant, Juan de Ayora, at Darien says: "In this expedition Juan de Ayora not only "omitted the requisitions and summoning which it was "his duty to make to the Indians before attacking them, "but took them by surprise at night, torturing the ca"ciques and chiefs, demanding gold from them. Some he "roasted alive, some were thrown living to the dogs, some "were hanged, and for others were designed new forms "of torture. Their wives and daughters were made slaves "and divided according to the pleasure of de Ayora and "the other captains."

These frightful cruelties did not take place without protest. The Dominican friar, Bartolomé de las Casas, whose contemporaneous account of the behaviour of his companions, taken with the histories recorded by Peter Martyr and Herrera, make what is probably the most

authentic record of the events and spirit of the time, de/
voted himself to the amelioration of the lot of the afflicted
Indians.

His accounts made a deep impression, not only in Spain,
but over the rest of Europe.* In 1542, because of his rep/
resentation to Carlos V, a royal commission was called to/
gether at Valladolid to devise a better system of govern/
ment for the West Indies. Many reforms were promulgated,
but few were enforced. Mixed with the stories of limit/
less treasure the piteous appeal of Las Casas reached Eng/
land and increased the hatred of Spain. During the last
half of the sixteenth century England began to play her
part in the Caribbean.

Frobisher, Davis, Gilbert, and others had gained re/
nown for themselves and territory for England in the
North. Hawkins, Drake, Raleigh, and the other great sea/
men and pioneers of Elizabethan England found ample
scope for their adventurous spirit to contest the claim of
Spain to dominion over the New World.

When Elizabethan England finally awoke to the call
of the New World, her navigators showed a daring and
persistency which made of England a gradually increas/
ing participator in the territory and wealth of the Carib/
bean. The narratives of the early voyages of Hawkins and
of Drake, minutely reported by them and by men of their

* *Breuissima Relación de la destruyción de las Indias.* By B. de las Casas
(1552).

companies, are not only crowded with the accounts of dangers overcome and battles fought, but are full of inter/esting descriptions of the lands visited and their inhabit/ants.

On his second voyage John Hawkins (afterwards Sir John Hawkins) left Plymouth in the autumn of 1564 with one ship of seven hundred tons, one of one hundred and forty tons, and two of fifty and thirty tons, respectively.

His total company consisted of one hundred and seventy men. He proceeded to the coast of Africa to take on board a cargo of negroes to be sold as slaves in the West Indies. It was not until March, 1565, that he touched at Domin/ica in the West Indies and at various smaller islands in that neighbourhood. He was not given a hospitable recep/tion, and the Spanish Viceroy at Hispaniola, advised of his arrival within the proscribed seas, directed that there should be no traffic with Hawkins, ordering the use of force against him if necessary.

At the small island of Cumana he was able to obtain provisions from the natives, whom he described as tract/able, and as excellent archers using arrows tipped with poison in warfare.

In April he touched the coast of Venezuela, but, fail/ing to secure a license to sell his negroes by friendly ne/gotiations, he landed one hundred men armed with " bows, "arrows, arquebuses and pikes," and marched toward the town of Barbarotta where the Spanish Governor was res/

ident. The local garrison was not prepared to resist and without actual fighting a permit to trade was obtained. From there he sailed along the coast to Cape Vela and to Rio de la Hacha. At this latter point another display of force was required to make it possible to trade. At the end of May he continued his voyage cruising around Jamaica, Cuba, and the Florida coast, arriving home some eleven months from the date of his departure from Plymouth.

Three years later, with the same flagship (the "Jesus "of Lubeck") and five smaller vessels, he again visited the West Indies with another and larger cargo of slaves. His difficulties had increased, however, because the King of Spain had himself forbidden traffic with Hawkins and the Spanish settlements were better prepared to resist him. At Rio de la Hacha he disposed of a part of his cargo ; but at Cartagena the resistance was too great for him to attempt to overcome it and he sailed thence for Florida. Storms drove him to seek shelter in one of the Mexican harbours from whence he only got away after many vi⁄cissitudes and much fighting with the Spanish garrison. Finally he returned home through the Bahamas.

With Hawkins on this last voyage, in command of the "Judith," had been Francis Drake. It is said that Drake a few years later was shown by Indians from a tree⁄top on the Isthmus of Panamá a view of the Pacific Ocean, and that he there and then resolved to be the first English⁄man to sail upon its waters. The voyage which he began in 1577 with a fleet of five vessels was destined to realize his ambition.

The account of this voyage, written by Francis Petty, one of Drake's crew, and included in Hakluyt's collection of "Voyages," is one which cannot fail to enliven the spirit of adventure in the most lethargic reader. After a stop at the Cape de Verde islands, he reached and explored the coast of Brazil, entered the River Plate, and proceeded southward to the Straits of Magellan. After passing through the Straits, he sailed northward along the coast, touching at the Peruvian ports all of which he found unfortified. Laden with rich booty, he determined to cross the Pacific, but first went as far north as California. He then accomplished the extraordinary feat of reaching home by rounding the Cape of Good Hope. The time required for the whole exploit was within a few days of three years.

In 1585, he began his great West Indian venture which included the looting of Cartagena to which incident a special chapter is devoted. Nine years after his return home from this undertaking, Drake and Hawkins jointly undertook the conquest of the Isthmus, a project which, their crews weakened by sickness, they were forced to abandon when, on arrival, they found the increased strength of the fortifications made the attempt useless.

This last was an unhappy voyage; Hawkins died off Puerto Rico and Drake off Puerto Bello. These two men were pioneers in the trade of legalized or commissioned piracy. Their example helped give birth to a new and virile band called "buccaneers," a name derived from the term applied to the sun/dried or bucan beef used by the filibusters to provision their vessels and which was dried on poles or slats called "bucans."

To secure to herself the full fruits of conquest, Spain, as has been noted, was resolved to exclude all foreigners. Rich as were the new countries in gold and other valua/ ble cargoes, the stories which reached Europe enlarged on facts which were in themselves enough to fire the envy and cupidity of the other nations. Quarrels based chiefly on differences of religion already had bred in England a hatred of Spain. The natural intolerance had been fanned to fever heat by the persecution of English sailors by the Spanish Inquisition. Intolerable cruelties were practised which encouraged reprisals. If to torture and burn here/ tics were an act of grace from the Spanish point of view, it was equally commendable on the part of an honourable English Protestant to scuttle a Papist ship or lay waste a Spanish settlement in the New World.

Up to the time of the defeat of the great Armada, Spain was powerful in home waters as well as in the West Indies, and the opportunities to successfully contest her supremacy in the Caribbean were few; but the defeat of the Armada in 1588 and the consequent decline of the sea/power of Spain opened the path across the sea.

United by a common antipathy to Spain and by an

universal and natural desire for gain, the adventurous seamen of England, France, and the Low Countries soon
made a formidable group determined to share in the rich
booty of the Spanish Main. In the beginning their acts
were those of ordinary piracy; but out of the heteroge-
neous band there developed in due course a half-organized,
semi-legalized horde of buccaneers who played an important if somewhat violent part in the contest for the supremacy of the Caribbean. Among these buccaneers or
filibusters were many men who displayed great ability, valour, and seamanship. Chivalry and worthy enterprise
were no less common than robbery and cruelty. Both the
great navigator and writer Dampier and Sir Henry Morgan were buccaneers, as were de Pointis and Du Casse.

The period during which the buccaneers were an important factor in lessening the power of Spain and increasing the authority of England in the New World extended
to the end of the seventeenth century; after the Treaty of
Ryswick in 1697, the opportunity for legitimate piracy
so seldom occurred that the calling no longer attracted
the great navigators, and those left soon turned into common rogues and murderers, the mere dregs of an association which had given a place in history to many great
names.

The name of Sir Walter Raleigh is so prominently associated with the settlement of Virginia that the part he
played in the West Indies is often overlooked. After the

failure of his first two attempts at colonization in Virginia, Raleigh in 1595, enticed by the successes of his country, men, planned an expedition to Guiana.

Guiana was the name given by the *Conquistadores* to the vast and unknown country forming the watershed of the Orinoco. Reference has already been made to the tales of fabulous beauty and richness of this unexplored region. Ordaz, an officer under Pizarro, had earned temporary fame by an apocryphal account of a great city which he claimed to have found, called Manoa, and ruled by a descendant of the Incas. Other travellers had even described its palace and temple as visible from the distance, but not actually reached by them. Almost coincident with the exploration by Raleigh early in 1595, Antonio de Berreo, the Spanish Governor of Trinidad, entered the region supposed to contain the great city of Manoa by way of Nueva Granada, and came down the Orinoco River. For almost a century the chimera of El Dorado influenced the explorations and inflamed the greed and animosities of the explorers of Nueva Granada and Guiana.

Raleigh's expedition was made up of five ships with a total of one hundred men. A large amount of the country was explored, but the mythical city was not found. The reports of these explorations are of great interest, but lack historical value on account of the constant confusion of the records of facts with the unconfirmed rumours to which the travellers gave credence.

Raleigh was successful, however, in overcoming the Spanish garrison at Trinidad and the coast towns, securing enough booty to encourage him to make further explorations. In the following year he explored the coast between the rivers Orinoco and Amazon; and it was not until 1617 that Raleigh finally gave up his hope to make of Guiana a rival of Mexico and Peru. In that year with a squadron of twelve ships he again sailed for Guiana, attacked and subdued San Tomé, but was obliged to return to England without the accomplishment of his object.

Spain laid claims upon King James on account of this attack by Raleigh, and despite the evidence that the latter had the full support of the King, Raleigh was sacrificed to what was believed to be political expediency and his expedition in effect disowned.

The history of Guiana was not finished, however; for years five nations fought for its control: Spain, Portugal, France, England, and Holland.

In the end it was divided among the five. The wars of rebellion ended the sovereignty of the first two; the other three still survive, interesting souvenirs of the early struggles.

The island of Jamaica, which in due course became the chief British possession in the West Indies, did not offer the same lure to the Spanish as did the islands of Cuba and Hispaniola and the mines of the Mainland. The island was, however, settled by the Spanish, with some

SPANIARDS DRIVEN TO CANNIBALISM BY HUNGER

(Theodore de Bry 1599)

admixture of Portuguese, and early in the sixteenth century St. Jago de la Vega, now Spanish Town, was founded
and became a city of some importance. At the close of
that century Sir Anthony Shirley landed a force, looted
the island, and burnt St. Jago de la Vega. Again, in 1643,
Captain William Jackson with three ships did some plundering; but it was not until an expedition consisting of
some thirty-eight ships and eight thousand men, under
Penn and Venables, attacked the island in 1655 that it was
actually conquered by the English.

Following Penn and Venables came Admiral Myngs,
and shortly afterwards Sir Henry Morgan, both of whom
used Jamaica as a base for their exploits.

The full history of explorations and settlements made
by the Spaniards and by the Elizabethan seamen in the
Caribbean Sea does not fall within the scope of this small
book. Its purpose is rather to indicate the general scope
of the early discoveries, the gradual development from a
region given over to a trade based on forced plundering to
an orderly and productive part of the world, and in particular to record those critical events which finally resulted
in the sea-mastery of the Caribbean by maritime England.

The adventure of Spain in exploring and colonizing
the New World has no parallel in history. It is unfortunate that the picture of her extraordinary triumphs is
blurred by the record of her cruelties; but the magnificent
result remains. During the one hundred and fifteen years

prior to the settlement of Jamestown in 1607, the whole of the West Indies, and the greater parts of South and Central Americas were brought under Spanish control, fortified cities built, and the various agencies of State and Church government installed.

The vice-regal establishments at Lima and in Mexico were second only to the Court at Madrid in brilliancy and magnificence. The fortifications at Cartagena, at Panamá, and in Hispaniola are of a size and strength which make of them to-day an indisputable record of marvellous accomplishment.

The Spanish temperament was not, however, fitted for the task to keep and foster what had been won. Rendered weak through over-confidence in her strength and through certain inherent faults of her own civilization, Spanish power in both the Old and New World was weakened, until finally in the nineteenth century the rebellion of her own colonies ended her dominion in the New World.

CHAPTER II

SIR FRANCIS DRAKE

WHEN Drake began his voyage around the world in 1577, Spain had the effective control of all of those parts of the American continents which had proven to be a source of wealth to Europe.

Protestant England under Elizabeth longed not only for a share of the rich plunder which the exploitation of the New World was gaining for Spain, but also for an opportunity to cross swords with Catholicism. On both sides the adventurous spirit was strangely mixed with re/ ligious enthusiasm. Prayers and piracy were closely, and often with sincerity, blended. The fact that no commerce except with Spain was permitted in the New World made trade by English ships and men possible only when carried on by privateers or armed vessels. The inevitable result of these conditions was that English ships ostensibly fitted for trade turned to plundering the rich galleons of Spain, giving rise to reprisals with terrible excesses on both sides.

Upon Drake's return from his great voyage around the world, begun in 1577 and ended in 1580, he was received with great enthusiasm by both Queen and country. On this voyage he had sacked the unguarded coast towns of Peru and Chili, and it is said returned with over half a million sterling of treasure taken chiefly from the Span/

ish possessions. That Drake himself was knighted and his company fêted by all England, was not unnaturally received as an insult by Philip, and added fuel to the flames of war already kindled. There could be now no further question of conciliating Spain, and every effort was made by Eliza/beth and her sailor counsellors to build up a naval estab/lishment of a strength equal to that of Philip, whose naval power had been almost doubled by the failure of the royal line of Portug ! which had brought the domination of that country under the Spanish Crown. To make havoc with the Spanish possessions in the New World appealed to both the political sagacity of the Queen and to the busi/ness/like judgment of those imbued with the buccaneer spirit of the age.

It has been necessary to refer again briefly to the gen/eral conditions affecting England and Spain at the time of the expedition against Cartagena and other towns of the Spanish Main, in order to understand the motives of an attack which has been variously described as a great legitimate naval expedition and as a series of wanton pirat/ical seizures.

Few men whose deeds have played such an important and forceful part in actual events, have had associated with their names so much of almost legendary romanticism as has that of Francis Drake. Knighted and made an admiral by Elizabeth, and dubbed a pirate by the Spaniards, he was in truth a mixture of the great soldier/admiral and the adventurous buccaneer. His father, Edmund Drake, is said to have been at one time a sailor, but whether this is true or not, it is certain that he had become vicar of Up⁄church, living near Tavistock, under the patronage of the Earl of Bedford. It was the earl's son, Francis Russell, v⸗o endowed the son born to Edmund Drake with his own name.

Francis Drake was born about 1545. His early associa⁄tions were strongly anti⁄Catholic. As a boy he was ap⁄prenticed to the master and owner of a small Channel coasting vessel, and appears to have been treated as a son by the master, who upon his death, which happened shortly, left the vessel to him.

Sir John Hawkins, said by some to have been a kins⁄man of Drake, had been early engaged in the slave⁄trade and in trading expeditions to the West Indies. In 1567, on his third expedition to which reference is made in the first chapter, he visited the Spanish Main, and succeeded in landing and selling his negroes at Rio de la Hacha only after overcoming armed resistance. He finally at Carta⁄gena abandoned this commerce. This voyage was in many respects unfortunate, and it was also alleged that many acts of bad faith on the part of the Spaniards brought great hardships, sufferings, and death to many of Hawkins's un⁄happy companions. Hawkins himself says in his account of the expedition: "If all the miseries and troublesome "affairs of this sorrowful voyage should be perfectly and "thoroughly written, there should need a painful man "with his pen, and as great a time as he had that wrote "the lives and deaths of the martyrs."

Great indignation was felt in England over the mis⁄ haps of this voyage and the treatment of the voyagers by the Spaniards. Drake had taken part in this expedition in command of the "Judith." He had previously sold his own little coaster and used the proceeds, with his other earnings, for the proper outfitting for this voyage with Hawkins. Drake lost everything in this unhappy venture, from which he barely escaped with his life, and became an ardent supporter of the doctrine, soon popular in England, that it was lawful to recover from the Spaniards that which their treachery had taken from the English traders.

In 1570, Drake again went to the West Indies, this time with two ships, the "Dragon" and the "Swan," and again in 1571 with the "Swan" alone. These voy⁄ ages appear to have been mainly to acquire information, or at least, that appears to have been their chief result. With the experience gained by these two voyages and the previous one with Hawkins, he sailed from Plymouth in May, 1572, with the "Pacha" of seventy tons, and "Swan" of twenty⁄five tons, with total crews of seventy⁄ three men and boys. By the end of July he reached Nom⁄ bre de Dios, and after a sharp but brief engagement, in which he himself was wounded, captured the town. From Nombre de Dios he sailed along the coast toward Carta⁄

gena, capturing several well-laden vessels on the way; but
making no stop of consequence until he arrived at the
Isthmus of Darien. There he found settlements of the
Cimarrones (or Maroons), negroes who had escaped from
slavery, with whom he entered into intercourse and by
the chief of whom he was shown, from a goodly and
" great high tree "on a commanding height, a sight of the
Pacific Ocean. Drake is reported to have " besought
" Almighty God of his goodness to give him life and leave
"to sail in an English ship on that sea." This same chief
guided and helped in an expedition overland to intercept
the trains of mules which brought treasure from Panamá
to Nombre de Dios. Beyond taking possession of a small
town on the road and destroying some property, the expedition appears to have been fruitless, and it was only
after great hardships and dangers that Drake and his men
regained their ships. He returned to Plymouth from this
voyage on August 9, 1573, somewhat enriched, but with
his ambition in no way satisfied. A valorous and venturesome seaman named John Oxenham, whose name is
closely associated with the stirring events of that day on
the Caribbean littoral, had served under Drake in this
expedition. About two years later, Oxenham, with one
ship and seventy men, retraced the course of Drake to Darien with the object of intercepting one of the richly laden mule trains from Panamá. He was informed by the
Cimarrones that the trains were now accompanied by a

strong guard, and abandoned this plan; but, helped by a few of the Cimarrones, he marched to the Pacific side, built himself a small pinnace, and gained the distinction of be' ing the first Englishman to sail upon the Pacific Ocean. In December, 1577, Drake started on his great trip of cir' cum'navigation, already referred to, with a fleet consist' ing of the " Pelican " and four smaller vessels, with a total complement of one hundred and sixty'four men. That the plans for this voyage had the full, if secret, concurrence of the Queen, there seems little doubt, notwithstanding the fact that one of its real if not avowed objects was to prey upon the colonies of a nation with which techni' cal peace existed. The story of this voyage has no place here, but its great success from both a naval and "profit' sharing " standpoint, and the enthusiasm with which the voyagers were received on their return in September, 1580, "richly fraught with gold, silver, silk, pearls, and " precious stones," added greatly to the prestige of Drake.

For the next four years Drake remained in England; he became Mayor of Plymouth for a brief period and then entered Parliament as member for Bossiney.

Early in 1585, Elizabeth could no longer blind herself to the certainty of the intention of Spain to attack Eng' land. A fleet of English ships laden with corn had been unfairly seized, and swift retribution was planned. Under letters of marque, Drake gathered about him at Plymouth the most formidable squadron of privateers ever brought together,* consisting of twenty-five ships with a total of twenty-three hundred sailors and soldiers. His vice-admi-

* The following is an extract from an account published by Thomas Cates, entitled: "A summarie and true discourse of Sir Francis Drake's West Indian voyage, begun in the yeere 1585."

This worthy knight for the service of his Prince and countrey having prepared his whole fleete, and gotten them down to Plimmouth in Devonshire, to the number of five and twenty saile of ships and pinnesses, and having assembled of souldiers and mariners, to the number of 2300 in the whole, embarked them and himselfe at Plimmouth aforesaid, the 12 day of September 1585, being accompanied with these men of name and charge, which hereafter follow:

Master Christopher Carleil Lieutenant General, a man of long experience in the warres as well by sea as land, who had formerly carried high offices in both kindes in many fights, which he discharged alwaies very happily, and with great good reputation.

Anthonie Powel Sergeant Major

Captaine Matthew Morgan, and Captaine John Sampson, Corporals of the field.

These officers had commandement over the rest of the land-Captaines, whose names hereafter follow:

Captaine Anthony Plat,	Captaine John Merchant,
Captaine Edward Winter,	Captaine William Cecill,
Captaine John Goring,	Captaine Walter Bigs,
Captaine Robert Pew,	Captaine John Hannam,
Captaine George Barton,	Captaine Richard Stanton.

Captaine Martine Frobisher Viceadmirall, a man of great experience in seafaring actions, who had caried the chiefe charge of many ships himselfe, in sundry voyages before, being now shipped in the Primrose.

Captaine Francis Knolles, Reereadmirall in the Galeon Leicester.

Master Thomas Vennor, Captaine in the Elizabeth Bonadventure under the Generall.

Master Edward Winter, Captaine in the Aide.

Master Christopher Carleil the Lieutenant generall, Captaine of the Tygar.

Henry White, Captaine of the sea Dragon.

Thomas Drake, Captaine of the Thomas.

Thomas Seelie, Captaine of the Minion.

Baily, Captaine of the Barke Talbot.

Robert Crosse, Captaine of the Bark Bond.

ral was the doughty Martin Frobisher; his rear-admiral, Francis Knollys; Lieutenant-General Christopher Carleill was in command of the ten companies of land troops included in the complement.

The fleet sailed from Plymouth on the twelfth of September, 1585. After threatening Bayona and Vigo, and by his promptness and courage doing much to injure the morale of the Spanish naval defences, Drake proceeded to the Cape de Verde Islands. There he took almost unopposed possession of the chief town, Santiago, and plundered the islands for provisions and anything of value. From there he began his voyage toward the West Indies with the greatest armament which had ever crossed the Atlantic. His plan was to weaken Spain by cutting off the chief sources of her wealth in the New World and to strengthen England by obtaining the mastery of the rich Caribbean ports from which it seemed a limitless stream of gold could be made to flow into the Old World.

During the voyage to the West Indies the men suffered severe losses from deaths due to an infectious sickness, and

George Fortescue, Captaine of the Barke Bonner.
Edward Carelesse, Captaine of the Hope.
James Erizo, Captaine of the White Lyon.
Thomas Moone, Captaine of the Vantage.
John Vaughan, Captaine of the Drake.
John Varney, Captaine of the George.
John Martin, Captaine of the Benjamin.
Edward Gilman, Captaine of the Skout.
Richard Hawkins, Captaine of the Galiot called the Ducke.
Bitfield, Captaine of the Swallow.

the squadron arrived somewhat weakened in consequence at the island of Dominica. This island is described by Thomas Cates, one of the company officers who wrote a complete account published in Hakluyt's " Voyages," as inhabited by " savage people, which goe all naked, "their skinne coloured with some painting of a reddish "tawny, very personable and handsome strong men." From thence the squadron proceeded toward Hispaniola (San Domingo), and spent Christmas (1585) at anchor at the island of St. Christopher (St. Kitts) where no people were found.

The city of San Domingo in Hispaniola was one of the chief strongholds of the Spaniards in the West Indies, and so strongly built and fortified that no serious attack had previously been attempted upon it. It was surrounded by walls and batteries of some strength and reputed to be garrisoned by a powerful force, although the Spanish accounts state that about two thousand only of the eight thousand inhabitants were capable of bearing arms and that in the actual defence of the city a few hundred only participated. Cates refers to the "glorious fame of the " citie of S. Domingo, being the ancientest and chiefe in' " habited place in all the tract of country thereabouts."

The squadron arrived at a safe landing place about ten miles from the city, on New Year's day, 1586, and not' withstanding the commotion created in the city by the approach of the large flotilla, the troops were secretly landed without molestation under cover of the night. On the morning following, Drake made a feint at landing on the opposite side toward which Carleill with the men already landed was approaching. The advantage gained by this manœuvre was pushed, and after a short engagement in the streets and market-place the victory was won.

The town was rather large for complete occupancy by the small number of troops under Carleill, and he was directed by Drake to entrench himself in the most substantial part of the town; the Spanish troops were in this way divided into two divisions, one which had fled to safety well outside of the city, and the other which remained in that part not invested by the English forces.

Drake now demanded a large ransom for the release of the town. During the negotiations he sent a negro boy with a flag of truce to the Spanish camp; the boy being met by a few Spanish officers was so wounded by one of them that he could barely crawl back within his own lines to die. This so inflamed the natural anger of Drake that in the first burst of his fury he caused to be hanged, on the spot of the boy's death, two friars who were among the prisoners; he declared that until the cowardly Spaniard who killed the boy was publicly executed two more prisoners would be hanged daily. This demand was quickly met. The amount of the ransom which the city, even with difficulty, could pay, was not so great as Drake had expected, and he had to be contented with twenty-five

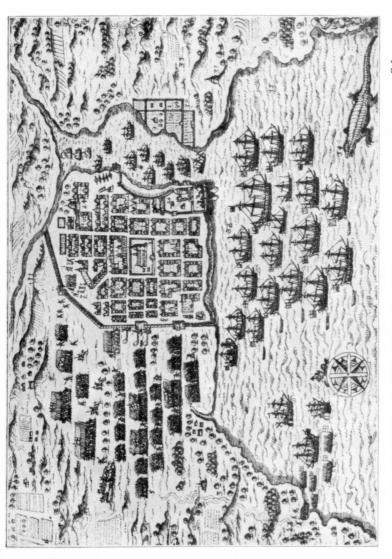

THE CAPTURE OF THE CITY OF SANTO DOMINGO BY DRAKE IN 1586

(Theodore de Bry, 1599)

thousand ducats, probably equivalent to about sixty thou/
sand dollars of American money. In addition, all valuable
property of a kind to permit of removal was taken aboard
the ships, including from two to three hundred guns and
ample stores of provisions. A few of the better vessels in
the harbor were taken and the remainder destroyed.

Exhilarated by victory, and with his squadron well
provisioned, Drake sailed the middle of February for Car/
tagena. It was now that the experience which he had
gained in his earlier voyages stood him in good stead, for
he could approach this difficult shore and harbour with
the confidence of an experienced pilot.

The town of Cartagena had been founded a little more
than fifty years before Drake's attack, and was already well
fortified, although its system of walls and fortifications
which were afterwards intended to make it impregnable,
were not then wholly completed. The town is situated a
few feet above sea/level at the eastern extremity of the
harbour or Bay of Cartagena. To the southwest it faces
the harbour, and to the northwest its long side is on the
edge of the open sea with the surf breaking near the base
of its strong walls. The remaining boundary is largely made
up of a great shallow lagoon almost connecting with the
sea on the one side, and connected with the harbour on
the other. The harbour itself is made nearly a closed ba/
sin by the island of Tierra Bomba, at each end of which in
Drake's time was an entrance for ships, the larger mouth,

called Boca Grande, the one nearer the city, and the smaller and more difficult mouth, called Boca Chica, at the western end of the bay.

The Boca Grande entrance was subsequently closed by artificial means, which, when once effected, was greatly helped by the natural drift of the sands. It has now been closed for all but the smallest boats for over two centuries.

Cartagena, by reason of its magnificent harbour and its nearness to the great river Magdalena, which leads down from the rich country in the interior, had become the storehouse of Spain in the New World, and the headquarters of all Spanish commerce. Philip had relied upon the reputation of Cartagena for strength to protect it from attack and had no conception that such an audacious attack upon his American possessions would be made; he had no time to send out reenforcements. So that although warned in advance of the impending visit of Drake with his formidable squadron, the Governor of Cartagena, Pedro Vique, could not depend on more than eleven or twelve hundred men all told for the defence of his city. This force was made up of fifty lancers, four hundred and fifty harquebusiers, one hundred pikemen, twenty negro musketeers, four hundred Indian bowmen, and one hundred and fifty harquebusiers who manned two galleys in the harbour.

The entrance to the inner harbour was defended by a fort at the place now called Pastelillo, but otherwise there

were no fortifications except those which surrounded the
city itself. The approach to the inner harbour was further
protected by chains, and the narrow neck of land reach
ing from the city to Boca Grande was defended by a stone
breastwork armed with a few guns and several hundred
men.

Drake entered through Boca Grande between three
and four o'clock in the afternoon without resistance. At
nightfall he landed the troops under the command of Car
leill close to Boca Grande. About midnight, having failed
to find paths through the thick growths which covered
the neck of land, they marched along the beach on the
side towards the sea, meeting only the slight resistance
offered by a small body of horsemen who retired at the
first volley.

The sound of this slight engagement was a signal to
Drake to carry out a prearranged plan, by which the ships
at once attacked the fort at the entrance to the inner har
bour. This attack was a diversion and was not pressed to a
successful conclusion, as indeed would have been difficult
in view of the narrowness of channel, the chains, and the
well sustained gun fire from the fort.

During this attack by the ships the troops pressed for
ward against the breastworks, which consisted of a strongly
built stone wall with a ditch without and flankings cover
ing every part. A small passing space was protected by
wine butts filled with earth, the whole mounted with six

guns and further protected by drawing up to the shore the two large galleys.

Carleill forced the attack on the space protected by the wine-butts, and largely through the superiority of the English pikes and armour a breach was made and quickly carried by storm. The defenders were forced into the city, where the streets were strongly barricaded. The Indians gave active help to the Spaniards, fighting with poisoned arrows and with small sharp poisoned sticks about eighteen inches long, and so placed in the ground that contact with the poisoned ends was difficult to avoid. Many of the Spanish leaders were killed and Drake was soon in possession of the city. Although Drake's idea had been to permanently hold Cartagena and use it for a base from which to attack the other Spanish settlements, the reduction which he had already suffered in his forces and the persistence of yellow fever among his men changed his plans, and he determined to exact the largest possible ransom and leave the place. At a general council of land captains* held at Cartagena on the twenty-seventh of

* Cates gives the text of the resolution adopted at this meeting as follows:

Whereas it hath pleased the Generall to demaund the opinions of his Captaines what course they thinke most expedient to be now undertaken, the Landcaptaines being asembled by themselves together, and having advised hereupon, doe in three points deliver the same.

The first, touching the keeping of the towne against the force of the enemie, either that which is present, or that which may come out of Spaine, is answered thus :

We holder opinion, that with this troope of men which we have presently with us in land-service, being victualled and munitioned, wee may well keepe the

February, it was resolved that it was inexpedient to pro⁄
ceed with the intended capture of Panamá and it was re⁄
solved to proceed home by the way of Florida.

towne, albeit that of men able to answere present service, we have not above
700. The residue being some 150 men by reason of their hurts and sicknesse
are altogether unable to stand us in any stead: wherefore hereupon the Sea-cap-
taines are likewise to give their resolution, how they will undertake the safetie
and service of the Shippes upon the arrivall of any Spanish Fleete.

The second poynt we make to be this, whether it bee meete to goe presently
homeward, or els to continue further tryall of our fortune in undertaking such
like enterprises as we have done already, and thereby to seeke after that bounti-
full masse of treasure for recompence of our travailes, which was generally expected at our comming forth of England: wherein we answere:

That it is well knowen how both we and the souldiers are entred into this action
as voluntarie men, without any imprest or gage from her Majestie or any body
els, and forasmuch as we have hitherto discharged the parts of honest men, so
that now by the great blessing and favour of our good God there have bin taken
three such notable townes, wherein by the estimation of all men would have been
found some very great treasures, knowing that S. Iago was the chiefe citie of all
the Islands and traffiques thereabouts, S. Domingo the chiefe citie of Hispaniola,
and the head government not only of that Iland, but also of Cuba, and of all
the Ilands about it, as also of such inhabitations of the firme land, as were next
unto it, & a place that is both magnificently builded, and interteineth great
trades of merchandise; and now lastly the citie of Cartagena, which cannot be
denied to be one of the chiefe places of most especiall importance to the Spaniard of all the cities which be on this side of the West India: we doe therefore
consider, that since all these cities, with their goods and prisoners taken in them,
and the ransoms of the said cities being all put together, are found farre short to
satisfie that expectation which by the generality of the enterprisers was first conceived: And being further advised of the slendernesse of our strengthe, where-
unto we be now reduced, as well in respect of the small number of able bodies,
as also not a litle in regard of the slacke disposition of the greater part of those
which remaine, very many of the better mindes and men being either consumed
by death, or weakened by sicknes and hurts: And lastly, since that as yet there
is not laid downe to our knowledge any such enterprise as may seeme convenient
to be undertaken with such few as we are presently able to make, and withall of
such certaine likelihoode, as with Gods good successe which it may please him

Drake demanded a ransom of one hundred thousand pounds, but this sum was declared by the Spaniards im⁄

to bestow upon us, the same may promise to yeeld us any sufficient contentment: We doe therefore conclude hereupon, that it is better to hold sure as we may the honour already gotten, and with the same to returne towards our gracious Soveraigne and Countrey, from whenece if it shall please her Majestie to set us foorth againe with her orderly meanes and intertainment, we are most ready and willing to goe through with anything that the uttermost of our strength and indevour shall be able to reach unto; but therewithal we doe advise, and protest that it is farre from our thoughts, either to refuse, or so much as to seeme to be wearie of any thing, which for the present, shalbe further required or directed to be done by us from our Generall.

The third and last poynt is concerning the ransome of this citie of Cartagena, for the which, before it was touched with any fire, there was made an offer of some xxviij. thousand pounds sterling.

Thus much we utter herein as our opinions agreeing (so it be done in good sort) to accept this offer aforesayde, rather then to break off by standing still upon our demaunds of one hundred thousand poundes, which seemes a matter impossible to bee performed for the present by them, and to say trueth, wee may now with much honour and reputation better be satisfied with that summe offered by them at the first (if they will now bee contented to give it) then we might at that time with a greal deale more, inasmuch as we have taken our full pleasure both in the uttermost sacking and spoyling of all their householde goods and marchandize, as also in that we have consumed and ruined a great part of their Towne with fire. And thus much further is considered herein by us, that as there bee in the Voyage a great many poore men, who have willingly adventured their lives and travailes, and divers amongst them having spent their apparell and such other little provisions as their small meanes might have given them leave to prepare, which being done upon such good and allowable intention as this action hath alwayes caried with it, meaning, against the Spanyard our greatest and most dangerous enemie: so surely we cannot but have an inward regarde so farre as may lye in us, to helpe either in all good sort towards the satisfaction of this their expectation, and by procuring them some little benefite to incourage them and to nourish this readie and willing disposition of theirs both in them and in others by their example against any other time of like occasion. But because it may bee supposed that herein wee forgette not the private benefite of our selves, and are thereby the rather mooved to incline our selves to this composition, wee doe therefore thinke good for the clearing of ourselves of all such sus-

possible to get together, and an amount equivalent to about twenty/eight thousand pounds was tendered. In the meantime, notwithstanding various courtesies exchanged between the higher officers on each side, much irritation appears to have arisen over the matter of the ransom, and a considerable part of the city was burned. Finally a ran/ som, stated by Cates to have been one hundred and ten thousand ducats, and by Spanish authorities to have been four hundred thousand dollars, was paid and the English troops evacuated. Drake, however, after leaving the city, appears to have insisted that an abbey or priory just out/ side had not been included in the terms of settlement, and continued to hold it until an additional sum of one thou/ sand crowns was paid.

The fleet had remained at Cartagena six weeks when it finally set sail the last of March. The voyage was de/ layed by leaky vessels, and the fleet did not arrive off Cape Anthony on the eastern end of Cuba until the twenty/ seventh of April. Here the fleet took water and proceeded

pition, to declare hereby, that what part or portion soever it bee of this ransome or composition for Cartagena, which should come unto us, wee doe freely give and bestowe the same wholy upon the poore men, who have remayned with us in the Voyage, meaning as well the Sayler as the Souldier, wishing with all our hearts it were such or so much as might seeme a sufficient rewarde for their paine- full indevour. And for the firme confirmation thereof, we have thought meete to subsigne these presents with our owne hands in the place and time aforesayd.

Captaine CHRISTOPHER CARLEILL *Lieutenant Generall*
Captaine GORING
Captaine SAMPSON
Captaine POWELL &c.

to the coast of Florida, where St. Augustine and various smaller and less important places were captured. The fleet then sailed for Plymouth and arrived there the twenty-eighth of July, 1586.

There were on this voyage a total of seven hundred and fifty men lost from all causes, the greater number from disease.

The total value of the booty gained was about sixty thousand pounds, not counting some two hundred and forty pieces of ordnance, of which about two hundred pieces were of brass, including sixty-three from Cartagena.

Drake had ably and bravely executed the task which had been given him and returned home with increased popularity and prestige. The actual injury to the King of Spain by the expedition was less than the harm done to individuals in the Spanish possessions, a fact which served to create a hatred of the English which survived for generations.

In the following year, 1587, when an invasion of England was again feared by Elizabeth, Drake was appointed to command the English fleet which was immediately formed to prevent the " joining together of the King of "Spain's fleet out of their several ports." He attacked Cadiz, where he destroyed thirty-three vessels and carried away others. After several other captures he returned to England, to be sent out again in July, 1588, as vice-admiral, under Lord Howard, of the fleet sent to intercept

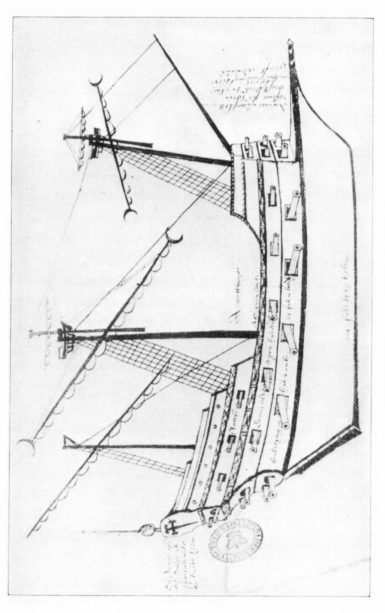

A SPANISH TREASURE FRIGATE

From a drawing by an English spy

the "Spanish Armada," the history of which adventure is well known.

The next year Drake was in command of an expedition to invade Spain and Portugal. After his return from this service, he again served in Parliament, but the sea once more claimed him in August, 1595, when he sailed for the West Indies, on what was to be his last voyage, with Sir John Hawkins as his vice-admiral. Hawkins died off Puerto Rico in November, and on the twenty-eighth of January, 1596, Drake himself died on board of his ship off Puerto Bello after a fortnight's illness in his cabin.

CHAPTER III

SIR HENRY MORGAN

IT has been shown in the earlier chapters how both by discovery and by conquest Spain in the sixteenth century claimed the exclusive right to the New World. Although this claim was successfully disputed by the English and French in the regions north of Florida, and by the Portuguese in certain other places, Spain had during the century following the first voyage of Columbus established her rule over the West Indies, Central America, and the greater part of the great continent to the south.

Tales of these vast and rich territories had bred in the venturesome hearts of many an Englishman and Frenchman a wish to share in the development and trade of this marvellous New World. Spain had clearly proclaimed, however, that all foreigners were forbidden entry to the waters of the Caribbean. Envy of the Spanish bred a hatred which was fanned to fever heat by the stories of cruelties inflicted on English sailors by their captors. The terror of the Inquisition at Cartagena had served in Protestant England to give a religious fervour to the hatred of Spain. This hatred was shared by the French and Dutch who wished for equal opportunities in the rich trade with the Caribbean Sea.

That the energy shown by Spain in colonizing and ex⁄ploring is without parallel in the records of such achieve⁄ments, has already been recorded. Panamá was crossed and the great empire of Peru was administered by a Spanish viceroy. In Mexico came the downfall of the Aztec em⁄pire. So advanced was the colonization of these two great vice⁄royalties that the University of San Marco was founded at Lima in 1551, and another University opened its doors in Mexico in 1553.

Spain suffered, however, from the over⁄confidence in⁄duced by her own greatness. Her exclusion of foreigners served to tie together her enemies in one common pur⁄pose. The name of Francis Drake had become the terror of the Spanish in the New World. To the hardy English mariners the profits of a trade in forbidden seas more than sufficed to balance its perils, while at home the most re⁄spectable persons thought anything a godly work which served to break up the Catholic monopoly of the New World. Drake's success lured the adventurous to the Carib⁄bean.

The defeat of the Spanish Armada in 1588 was a blow to the sea⁄power of Spain. Her naval supremacy was lost. Without the command of the seas an empire widely scat⁄tered and separated by broad expanses of oceans could not be held intact. The time had come for the great Protest⁄ant power, England, to take her part in the development of the New World. The growth of English trade and the increase in her shipping were still further stimulated by the long peace during the reign of Charles I.

The Continental wars had been profitable to England; her ships were thrusting themselves into every trade, and her manufactures prospering. The failure of the Virginian settlement of Raleigh had been followed by the more successful undertaking of John Smith. The Pilgrim Fathers had settled on the New England coast. The civil war and the government of Cromwell delayed somewhat the spread of English influence and control in the West Indies and the Spanish Main. Cromwell, the Puritan, however, could not but share the old English hatred of the great Papist state, and over his own hand wrote to his admirals in the West Indies, "the Lord Himself hath a controversy with "your enemies; even with that Romish Babylon of which "the Spaniard is the great under-propper. In that respect "we fight the Lord's battles."

Early in 1655, although no war had actually been declared between England and Spain, one English fleet under Blake failed in an attempt to intercept a Spanish treasure fleet from the West Indies, but another expedition, although failing to capture San Domingo, seized and held the island of Jamaica. These acts naturally resulted in actual war with Spain and later in the same year Cromwell signed a treaty of alliance with France.

This capture of Jamaica by the English was the first permanent occupation by a power other than Spain in that part of the New World.

A cessation of hostilities followed the restoration of
the monarchy, and on the accession of Charles II, in May,
1660, negotiations intended to lead to a permanent peace
and the re-establishment of commercial relations were
inaugurated. This armistice or peace appears to have been
somewhat doubtfully interpreted in the West Indies. It
was generally construed not to include the New World,
but to apply to Europe only. None of the difficulties of
trade had been settled and with such conflicting interests
and aims any real peace in the Caribbean was impossible.

In January, 1664, Sir Thomas Modyford, then Governor of Barbadoes, was appointed Governor of Jamaica.
By the instructions given him, dated February, 1664, he
was directed to encourage trade and friendly relations with
the Spanish Dominion and to prohibit the granting of letters of marque. It was not until June, however, that Modyford arrived in Jamaica and proclaimed a cessation of
hostilities. Neither this proclamation nor the polite communication which he sent to the neighbouring Spanish
Governor at Cartagena was sufficient to accomplish actual
good relations. A few days before his arrival, the temporary President of the Jamaica Council had written, "It is
"not in the power of the governor to have or suffer a
"commerce, nor will any necessity or advantage bring
"private Spaniards to Jamaica, for we and they have used
"too many mutual barbarisms to have a sudden corre-
"spondence." The fact that the chief cause of the trou-

ble, the buccaneers, were still active made the task of Modyford more difficult.

This much of the general conditions precedent to the participation of Sir Henry Morgan in the operations of the English in the Caribbean Sea has been necessary to record in order to view in proper perspective the character and exploits of this variously regarded but certainly remarkable man.

It will be wise to consider even more intimately the actual conditions in the West Indies in order to judge fairly, and with proper regard to the exigencies of the moment, the exact part played by Sir Henry Morgan both in encouraging and afterwards in suppressing the buccaneers.

The bearer to the West Indies of the commission and instructions to Modyford had been Colonel Edward Morgan, an uncle of Sir Henry Morgan. Colonel Morgan had been named as Sir Thomas Modyford's deputy-governor, and appears to have shown zeal in furthering by acts the instructions of which he had been the bearer.

The island of Tortuga was the principal rendezvous of the buccaneers. At this time French influence was in the ascendant in the mixed colony at Tortuga, and it is not strange that no sympathy was felt with the avowed English design of bringing to an end the highly remunerative "trade" of the buccaneers. The controlling spirit in the colony was Bertrand d'Ogeron, the representative, with title of governor, sent out by the French West-India Company.

Not only was the conquest of Tortuga necessary if the buccaneers were to be effectively suppressed, but the many less organized and roving buccaneers, who refused to give up their commissions or licenses must needs be searched out and forced to obedience. Modyford was almost pow-erless, however, as King Charles had recalled from the West Indies practically all English men-of-war, while on the other hand the buccaneers had increased in numbers. It was estimated that nearly two thousand men from Ja-maica alone, in some fourteen or fifteen different ships, were engaged in the business.

In the early spring of 1665, Modyford, having first obtained permission from home, despatched Colonel Ed-ward Morgan with five hundred men and ten ships to attack first the Dutch trading at St. Kitts or St. Eustatius, then to visit Tortuga and Hispaniola. Hostilities between the Dutch and English had been expected for some time.

Colonel Morgan, although described by Modyford in his report of the setting forth of this expedition as an "honest privateer," appears to have had some difficulty in controlling the rabble of which his crews were com-posed. It is to be remembered that Jamaica at this time was largely colonized from the prisons of England and by roughs and vagrants of all kinds, to whom the gentle-manly profession of privateering strongly appealed.

At St. Eustatius Colonel Morgan landed with a some/ what diminished body of followers, and attacked the Dutch garrison, who were fairly well placed in a fort of some strength on an eminence. For some reason, which does not appear in the record, the Dutch Governor surrendered without the strong opposition which was to have been expected. Colonel Morgan, however, then well along in years and unfitted for this sort of service, died during this action. The plunder was substantial, but in the quarrels of the crews and the subsequent dispositions made we are not now concerned. Colonel Morgan, the uncle of Sir Henry, appears to have had the respect and confidence of his King and countrymen.

In the autumn of the same year, Modyford, anxious to pursue the design interrupted by the death of Colonel Morgan, called to his aid one of the most noted of the privateers of the time, Captain Edward Mansfield. Blue/ fields Bay on the Central American coast was named as a rendezvous for the buccaneers. A state of actual war ex/ isted between the Dutch and the English, and shortly af/ ter this France, rallying to the support of her allies, the Dutch, declared war against England. It became a mat/ ter of urgent policy for Modyford to attract the bucca/ neers from their French associates. The original orders to Modyford were modified, and the granting of commis/ sions, or letters of marque, was left to his discretion. In a way matters were not seriously affected by this change

of attitude on the part of the English Government because the buccaneers had continued — although not legally
commissioned so to do — to prey upon the Spanish settlements and commerce ; but with the legalization of the
expedition under Mansfield, the ports of Jamaica were
opened for the disposal of booty and the refitting of ships.

A few months before Mansfield left Jamaica for the
appointed rendezvous, it is reported that Henry Morgan
and two other privateer captains had come to Port Royal
with tales of great wealth in Central America. In January
of 1665, Henry Morgan and his two associates, Jackman
and Morris, had explored and plundered part of the province of Campeache, an expedition to which further reference will be made, and there appears little doubt that
Henry Morgan accompanied Mansfield on his expedition
— possibly, as Exquemelin states, as his " Vice-Admiral."

Mansfield's fleet had an adventurous and prosperous
voyage. He plundered somewhat in Cuba, captured Providence Island, sacked Granada, the capital of Nicaragua,
and plundered Costa Rica as far inland as Turrialba.
Somewhat worn by long land journeys, they gave up the
uphill march to Cartago and passed out through Veragua,
where they joined their ships, which, deeply laden with
booty, they sailed into Port Royal, Jamaica. Mansfield
had exceeded his orders, but appears to have been more
commended than reproved. He was soon afterwards
engaged in the defence of Providence, which his energy

had made an English island, and in some way came to his death.

From now on Henry Morgan became a commanding figure in the West Indies. The circumstances were fitted for the fullest development of a man of his daring, resourceful, and not too scrupulous character.

Henry Morgan was almost certainly born in Monmouthshire, about 1635; according to his own statement he was the son of a gentleman, but there is little evidence bearing on his birth and parentage other than his own declarations made from time to time; there appears however no reason to doubt that he came from respectable Welsh stock. Of his father little is known, but that his uncle, Colonel Edward Morgan, was a trusted and somewhat distinguished servant of the Crown we have, as has been shown, positive knowledge. It is known that at about the age of thirty, Henry Morgan married his first cousin, a daughter of his uncle, Colonel Edward Morgan. Colonel Morgan's wife was the daughter of a Saxon nobleman, Baron von Pölnitz. The great popular knowledge of Henry Morgan and interest in him is derived from a History of the Buccaneers written by one John Exquemelin * and first published in Dutch at Amsterdam in the year

* Little is positively known of Exquemelin. He is variously described as a Frenchman, Hollander, and Fleming. The fact that the first edition of his account is in Dutch throws doubt on the suggestion of French birth. He is first known as a servant of the French West India Company at Tortuga; afterwards he joined the buccaneers and was one of the followers of Morgan in several expeditions. (The Dutch spelling of his name has been adopted except in quoted matter.)

BUCANIERS

O F

A M E R I C A:

Or, a true

ACCOUNT

O F T H E

Moſt remarkable Aſſaults

Ccmmitted of late years upon the Coaſts of

The West-Indies,

By the Bucaniers of *Jamaica* and *Tortuga*,
Both *E N G L I S H* and *F R E N C H.*

Wherein are contained more eſpecially,

The unparallel'd Exploits of Sir *Henry Morgan,* our Engliſh *Jamaican* Hero, who ſack'd *Puerto Velo,* burnt *Panama,*&c.

Written originally in *Dutch,* by *John Eſquemeling,* one of the
Bucaniers, who was preſent at thoſe Tragedies ; and thence
tranſlated into *Spaniſh,* by *Alonſo de Bonne-maiſon,* Doctor of
Phyſick, and Practitioner at *Amſterdam.*
Now faithfully rendred into *Engliſh.*

L O N D O N:

Printed for *William Crooke,* at the Green Dragon without *Temple-bar.* 1 6 8 4.

1678. It was almost immediately translated and published in German and in Spanish (1681); from the Spanish edition it was translated into English and published by W. Crooke, in London in 1684, with the accompanying titlepage.

In the same year another translation was also issued in London by Thomas Malthus, which differs in some particulars from the translation issued by Crooke, and purports to include the testimony of other eyewitnesses.

Exquemelin's account of Morgan described him as more of a pirate than a commissioned privateer, and attributed to him cruel and unnecessary acts, which greatly incensed Morgan and his friends. Malthus was brought immediately into court under charge of libel, and a record of the case is one of the interesting sources of information regarding Morgan, who won the suit. Influenced probably by the difficulties of Malthus, William Crooke published a second edition with an explanatory although apparently not sufficiently apologetic preface, as it was later followed by a vastly entertaining and almost mawkish public apology to which reference will again be made. These records, taken with the Minutes of the Council Books of Jamaica, and the long files of correspondence between Morgan and the Lords of Trade and Plantations and other London officials, make on the whole a fairly convincing record of the character and exploits of Sir Henry Morgan.

According to Exquemelin, a statement for which the
publisher Malthus suffered and Crooke apologized, Mor/
gan was kidnapped when a boy and sold as an indentured
servant in Barbadoes. Morgan, who appears to have been
particularly sensitive as to this story, always stoutly denied
it. In any event, either involuntarily or by deliberate intent
he went as a youth to Barbadoes and in due course, as a
young man to Jamaica, where he joined the buccaneers.
His capacity and talent for command soon made him cap/
tain of a ship.

Words which not so long ago were understood by
every one are to/day used so carelessly that it may be well
to remind the reader that a buccaneer or privateer is not
necessarily a pirate. The privateers were always, or sup/
posedly always, commissioned by some appropriate gov/
ernmental authority. A pirate has, of course, no license
or authority save from his own strength, courage, and
wit.

There is some doubt as to whether the commission
under which they sailed was still valid or had expired, but
early in 1665, Morgan and two other privateer captains,
Jackman and Morris, had, as has been before recorded,
carried out a profitable venture in Central America. With
over one hundred followers they had left their ships
at the mouth of the Tabasco River in Campeache, and
guided by friendly Indians they reached and sacked the
town called Villa de Mosa, a trading centre some thirty/

five miles above the mouth. On their return they found their ships had been seized by Spaniards whose numbers exceeded theirs some threefold. The hardy buccaneers, however, were more than a match for the less robust land soldiers and soon drove off the Spaniards. They then fitted boats appropriate for the service, and sailed off, and cap/ tured and plundered both Rio Garta and Truxillo. From there they passed down the Mosquito Coast, plundering everything worth while, and finally made Monkey Bay their base for operations in Nicaragua. They appear to have been much impressed with the climate and beauty of Lake Nicaragua, the one/hundred/mile journey to which they had made in canoes up the San Juan River. By an adroitly conceived and brilliantly executed night attack on the city of Granada, they seized the magazines and principal big guns within the actual city and locked up in the cathedrals several hundred of the more prosper/ ous citizens. For over half a day they plundered the town, and then, after rendering useless all boats except those needed for their own return to the coast, they opened the doors of the cathedrals and released their prisoners.*

The lure of climate, scenery, and an easily looted city appears to have been irresistible, because it will be re/ membered that it was only a year afterwards that Mans/

---

* Except for some variations in geographical names used, a not uncommon fault with the contemporaneous accounts of these days, the principal facts of this visit are confirmed by the report of the Viceroy of New Spain.

field, with Henry Morgan as one of his captains — and presumably his vice-admiral — again attacked and looted the city of Granada.

If there was really any doubt as to the validity of the commission under which Morgan and his associates had sailed, their acts certainly appear to have been fully ap-proved or at least condoned. In the absence of and after the death of Mansfield, Sir Thomas Modyford, being without support of any proper naval establishment, called upon Morgan to assist in protecting the island of Jamaica from an expected invasion by the Spaniards, and commis-sioned him to get the English privateers together with a view to take some Spanish prisoners and learn from them the actual intentions and strength of the enemy. It must be said of young Captain Morgan, then but thirty-three years old, that his courage in construing orders and com-missions was not even exceeded by his dauntless energy and bravery when engaged with the enemy. He looked at the intent rather than at the letter of his instructions, a course which experience has shown is forgiven and jus-tified by success — and by that only.

Exquemelin's story of Morgan's next expedition is dis-puted by Morgan himself in so few of its essentials, and is so full of the flavour of the irresponsible and stirring times in which the events happened, that generous quo-tations of a portion of his narrative may well be made. It is to be borne in mind, however, that the allegations of extreme cruelty were hotly denied by Morgan and his friends, a fact which will be considered later.

"Captain Morgan who always communicated Vigour "with his words, infused such Spirits into his men, as "were able to put every one of them instantly upon new "designs: They being all perswaded by his Reasons, that "the sole execution of his Orders, would be a certain means "of obtaining great Riches. This perswasion had such "influence upon their minds that with unimitable Cour⁄ "age they all resolved to follow him. The same likewise "did a certain Pirat of Campeche; who in this ocasion "joyned with Captain Morgan, to seek new fortunes un⁄ "der his conduct, and greater advantages than he had "found before. Thus Captain Morgan, in few days, gath⁄ "ered a Fleet of nine sail, between Ships and great Boats; "wherein he had four hundred and threescore military "men.

"After that all things were in a good posture of readi⁄ "ness, they put forth to Sea, Captain Morgan imparting "the design he had in his mind unto no body for that "present. He onely told them on several occasions, that, "he held as indubitable, he should make a good fortune "by that Voyage, if strange occurrences altered not the "course of his designs. They directed their course to⁄ "wards the Continent; where they arrived in few days "upon the Coast·of Costa Rica, with all their Fleet entire. "No sooner had they discovered Land, but Captain Mor⁄

"gan declared his intentions to the Captains, and pres⁄
"ently after unto all the rest of the Company. He told
"them, he intended in that Expedition to plunder Puerto
"Velo, and that he would perform it by night, being re⁄
"solved to put the whole City to the sack, not the least
"corner escaping his diligence. Moreover, to encourage
"them, he added, This Enterprize could not fail to suc⁄
"ceed well, seeing he had kept it secreet in his mind,
"without revealing it to any body ; whereby they could
"not have notice of his coming. Unto this proposition
"some made answer, They had not a sufficient number
"of men wherewith to assault so strong and great a City.
"But Captain Morgan replied, If our number is small, our
"hearts are great. And the fewer persons we are, the
"more union and better shares we shall have in the spoil.
"Hereupon, being stimulated with the ambition of those
"vast Riches they promised themselves from their good
"success, they unanimously concluded to venture upon
"that design. But now, to the intent my Reader may bet⁄
"ter comprehend the incomparable boldness of this Ex⁄
"ploit, it may be necessary to say something before⁄hand
"of the City of Puerto Velo.

    "The City, which beareth this name in America, is
"seated in the Province of Costa Rica, under the altitude
"of ten degrees Northern latitude, at the distance of four⁄
"teen leagues from the Gulf of Darien, and eight West⁄
"wards from the Port called Nombre de Dios. It is judged

SIR HENRY MORGAN

"to be the strongest place that the King of Spain pos-
"sesseth in all the West-Indies, excepting two, that is to
"say, Havana and Cartagena. Here are two Castles, almost
"inexpugnable, that defend the City, being situated at the
"entry of the Port; so that no Ship nor Boat can pass with-
"out permission. The Garrison consisteth of three hun-
"dred Souldiers, and the Town constantly inhabited by
"four hundred Families, more or less. The Merchants
"dwell not here, but onely reside for a while, when the
"Galeons come or go from Spain; by reason of the un-
"healthiness of the Air, occasioned by certain Vapours
"that exhale from the Mountains. Notwithstanding, their
"chief Ware-houses are at Puerto Velo, howbeit their
"Habitations be all the year long at Panama. From
"whence they bring the Plate upon Mules, at such
"times as the Fair beginneth; and when the Ships, be-
"longing to the Company of Negro's, arrive here to sell
"Slaves.

    "Captain Morgan, who knew very well all the Ave-
"nues of this City, as also all the Neighbouring Coasts,
"arrived in the dusk of the Evening at the place called
"Puerto de Naos, distant ten Leagues towards the West
"of Puerto Velo. Being come unto this place, they
"mounted the River in their Ships, as far as another Har-
"bour called Puerto Pontin; where they came to an An-
"chor. Here they put themselves immediately into Boats
"and Canows, leaving in the Ships onely a few men to

"keep them, and conduct them the next day unto the
"Port. About midnight they came to a certain place
"called Estera longa Lemos, where they all went on
"shore, and marched by land to the first Posts of the City.
"They had in their company a certain English⁄man, who
"had been formerly a Prisoner in those parts, and who
"now served them for a Guide. Unto him and three or
"four more, they gave Commission to take the Centry,
"if possible, or kill him upon the place. But they laid
"hands on him and apprehended him with such cunning,
"as he had no time to give warning with his Musket, or
"make any other noise. Thus they brought him, with
"his hands bound, unto Captain Morgan, who asked him,
"How things went in the City, and what Forces they
"had: with many other circumstances, which he was de⁄
"sirous to know. After every question, they made him a
"thousand menaces to kill him, in case he declared not
"the truth. Thus they began to advance towards the City,
"carrying always the said Centry bound before them.
"Having marched about one quarter of a league, they
"came unto the Castle that is nigh unto the City; which
"presently they closely surrounded, so that no person
"could get either in or out of the said Fortress.

"Being thus posted under the walls of the Castle, Cap⁄
"tain Morgan commanded the Centry, whom they had
"taken Prisoner, to speak unto those that were within,
"charging them to surrender, and deliver themselves up

"to his discretion; otherwise they should be all cut in
"pieces, without giving quarter to any one. But they
"would hearken to none of these threats, beginning in⁄
"stantly to fire; which gave notice unto the City, and this
"was suddenly alarm'd. Yet notwithstanding, although
"the Governour and Souldiers of the said Castle made as
"great resistance as could be performed, they were con⁄
"strained to surrender unto the Pirats. These no sooner
"had taken the Castle, but they resolved to be as good
"as their words, in putting the Spaniards to the Sword,
"thereby to strike a terrour into the rest of the City.
"Hereupon, having shut up all the Souldiers and Officers,
"as Prisoners, into one Room, they instantly set fire unto
"the Powder (whereof they found great quantity) and
"blew up the whole Castle into the air, with all the
"Spaniards that were within. This being done, they pur⁄
"sued the course of their Victory, falling upon the City,
"which as yet was not in order to receive them. Many of
"the Inhabitants cast their precious Jewels and Moneys
"into Wells and Cisterns, or hid them in other places
"under ground, to excuse, as much as were possible, their
"being totally robb'd. One party of the Pirats being as⁄
"signed to this purpose, ran immediately to the Cloisters,
"and took as many Religious men and women as they
"could find. The Governour of the City not being able
"to rally the Citizens, through the huge confusion of the
"Town, retired unto one of the Castles remaining, and

"from thence began to fire incessantly at the Pirats. But
"these were not in the least negligent either to assault
"him, or defend themselves with all the courage imagi⁄
"nable. Thus it was observable, that amidst the horrour of
"the Assault, they made very few shot in vain. For aim⁄
"ing with great dexterity at the mouths of the Guns, the
"Spaniards were certain to lose one or two men every
"time they charged each Gun anew.

"The assault of this Castle where the Governour was,
"continued very furious on both sides, from break of day
"until noon. Yea, about this time of the day, the case was
"very dubious which party should conquer or be con⁄
"quered. At last the Pirats perceiving they had lost many
"men, and as yet advanced but little towards the gaining
"either this or the other Castles remaining, thought to
"make use of Fire⁄balls, which they threw with their
"hands, designing, if possible, to burn the doors of the
"Castle. But going about to put this in execution, the Span⁄
"iards from the Walls let fall great quantity of stones, and
"earthen pots full of Powder, and other combustible mat⁄
"ter, which forced them to desist from that attempt. Cap⁄
"tain Morgan seeing this generous defence made by the
"Spaniards, began to despair of the whole success of the
"Enterprize. Hereupon many faint and calm meditations
"came into his mind ; neither could he determine which
"way to turn himself in that straitness of affairs. Being
"involved in these thoughts, he was suddenly animated

"to continue the assault, by seeing the English Colours
"put forth at one of the lesser Castles, then entred by
"his men. Of whom he presently after spied a Troop that
"came to meet him, proclaiming Victory with loud shouts
"of joy. This instantly put him upon new resolutions of
"making new efforts to take the rest of the Castles that
"stood out against him: Especially seeing the chiefest
"Citizens were fled unto them, and had conveyed thither
"great part of their Riches, with all the plate belonging
"to the Churches, and other things dedicated to Divine
"Service.

  "Unto this effect therefore he ordered ten or twelve
"Ladders to be made, in all possible haste, so broad, that
"three or four men at once might ascend by them. These
"being finished, he commanded all the Religious men and
"women whom he had taken Prisoners, to fix them
"against the Walls of the Castle. Thus much he had be⁄
"fore⁄hand threatned the Governour to perform, in case
"he delivered not the Castle. But his answer was, He
"would never surrender himself alive. Captain Morgan
"was much perswaded that the Governour would not
"employ his utmost Forces, seeing Religious women,
"and Ecclesiastical persons, exposed in the Front of the
"Souldiers to the greatest dangers. Thus the Ladders,
"as I have said, were put into the hands of Religious
"persons of both Sexes; and these were forced, at the
"head of the Companies, to raise and apply them to the

"Walls. But Ca⸱ ⸱n Morgan was fully deceived in his
"judgment of this desig⸱⸱. For the Governour, who acted
"like a brave and couragious Souldier, refused not, in
"performance of his duty, to use his utmost endeavours
"to destroy whosoever came near the Walls. The Reli⸍
"gious men and women ceased not to cry unto him and
"beg of him by all the Saints of Heaven, he would de⸍
"liver the Castle, and hereby spare both his and their own
"lives. But nothing could prevail with the obstinacy and
"fierceness that had possessed the Governour's mind. Thus
"many of the Religious men and Nuns were killed be⸍
"fore they could fix the Ladders. Which at last being
"done, though with great loss of the said Religious peo⸍
"ple, the Pirats mounted them in great numbers, and with
"no less valour; having Fire⸍balls in their hands, and
"Earthen⸍pots full of Powder. All which things, being
"now at the top of the Walls, they kindled and cast in
"among the Spaniards.

"This effort of the Pirats was very great : Insomuch as
"the Spaniards could no longer resist nor defend the Castle,
"which was now entred. Hereupon they all threw down
"their Arms, and craved quarter for their lives. Onely the
"Governour of the City would admit nor crave no mercy;
"but rather killed many of the Pirats with his own hands,
"and not a few of his own Souldiers, because they did
"not stand to their Arms. And although the Pirats asked
"him if he would have quarter, yet he constantly an⸍

"swer'd, By no means: I had rather die as a valiant Soul⁄
"dier, than be hanged as a Coward. They endeavoured,
"as much as they could, to take him Prisoner. But he
"defended himself so obstinately, as that they were forced
"to kill him; notwithstanding all the cries and tears of
"his own Wife and Daughter, who begged of him upon
"their knees he would demand quarter and save his life.
"When the Pirats had possessed themselves of the Castle,
"which was about night, they enclosed therein all the
"Prisoners they had taken, placing the women and men
"by themselves, with some Guards upon them. All the
"wounded were put into a certain apartment by it self,
"to the intent their own complaints might be the cure
"of their diseases; for no other was afforded them.

"This being done, they fell to eating and drinking,
"after their usual manner; that is to say, committing in
"both these things all manner of debauchery and excess.
"These two vices were immediately followed by many
"insolent actions of Rape and Adultery committed upon
"many very honest women, as well married as Virgins:
"Who being threatned with the Sword, were constrained
"to submit their bodies to the violence of those lewd and
"wicked men. After such manner they delivered them⁄
"selves up unto all sort of debauchery of this kind, that
"if there had been found onely fifty courageous men, they
"might easily have retaken the City, and killed all the
"Pirats. The next day, having plundred all they could find,

"they began to examine some of the Prisoners (who had
"been perswaded by their Companions to say, they were
"the richest of the Town) charging them severely, to dis-
"cover where they had hidden their Riches and Goods.
"But not being able to extort anything out of them, as
"who were not the right persons that possessed any wealth,
"they at last resolved to torture them. This they per-
"formed with such cruelty, that many of them died upon
"the Rack, or presently after. Soon after, the President
"of Panama had news brought him of the pillage and
"ruine of Puerto Velo. This intelligence caused him
"to employ all his care and industry to raise Forces,
"with design to pursue and cast out the Pirats from
"thence. But these cared little for what extraordinary
"means the President used, as having their Ships nigh at
"hand, and being determined to set fire unto the City,
"and retreat. They had now been at Puerto Velo fifteen
"days, in which space of time they had lost many of their
"men, both by the unhealthiness of the Country and the
"extravagant Debaucheries they had committed.

  "Hereupon they prepared for a departure, carrying on
"Board their Ships all the Pillage they had gotten. But
"before all, they provided the Fleet with sufficient Vict-
"uals for the Voyage. While these things were getting
"ready, Captain Morgan sent an Injunction unto the Pris-
"oners, that they should pay him a Ransom for the City,
"or else he would by fire consume it to ashes, and blow

"up all the Castles into the air. Withal, he commanded
"them to send speedily two persons to seek and procure
"the sum he demanded, which amounted unto one hun-
"dred thousand pieces of Eight. Unto this effect, two
"men were sent to the President of Panama, who gave
"him an account of all these Tragedies. The President
"having now a body of men in a readiness, set forth im-
"mediately towards Puerto Velo to encounter the Pirats
"before their retreat. But these People hearing of his
"coming, instead of flying away went out to meet him
"at a narrow passage, through which of necessity he
"ought to pass. Here they placed an hundred men very
"well arm'd; the which, at the first Encounter, put to
"flight a good party of those of Panama. This Accident
"obliged the President to retire for that time, as not be-
"ing yet in a posture of strength to proceed any farther.
"Presently after this Rencounter, he sent a Message unto
"Captain Morgan, to tell him, That in case he departed
"not suddenly with all his Forces from Puerto Velo, he
"ought to expect no quarter for himself nor his Compan-
"ions, when he should take them, as he hoped soon to
"do. Captain Morgan, who feared not his Threats, as
"knowing he had a secure retreat in his Ships which
"were nigh at hand, made him answer, He would not
"deliver the Castles before he had received the Contri-
"bution-money he had demanded. Which in case it were
"not paid down, he would certainly burn the whole City,

"and then leave it; demolishing before hand the Castles,
"and killing the Prisoners."

According to Exquemelin's account, the Governor
of Panamá decided that further efforts on behalf of the
people of Puerto Bello would be unavailing and he left the
citizens to their own resources. Whether this is true, or
whether, as Morgan states, the ransom was paid by the
"President of Panamá" or by the citizens themselves, it
appears certain that the large sum of one hundred thousand pieces of eight was delivered to Morgan. The Governor of Panamá appears to have had some sportsmanlike
qualities, however, and Morgan a grim sense of humour,
because the former, impressed by the effectiveness of the
arms used by Morgan's men, sent a messenger to him to
ask for a "pattern of those arms wherewith he had taken
"with such violence so great a city." Captain Morgan
received the messenger with great civility and sent by him
to the Governor a pistol with a few bullets and a message
to the effect that "He desired him to accept that slender
"pattern of the arms wherewith he had taken Porto Bello,
"and keep them for a twelvemonth, after which time,
"he promised to come to Panama and fetch them away."
The pistol was returned with a courteous suggestion that
Captain Morgan, if he did come, would not fare so well
as he had at Puerto Bello.

After loading on his ships the best of the guns from
the fortifications and spiking the rest, Morgan proceeded

with his ships to a quiet harbour on the coast of Cuba and made distribution of the booty gathered on this ex⁄pedition. If the value at that time of a dollar of to⁄day is taken into consideration, the amount divided was an enor⁄mous sum, amounting to some two hundred and fifty thousand pieces of eight, equivalent in purchasing value to⁄day to approximately one million American dollars. The value of the cloths, silks, and other merchandise taken was also considerable in nearly all of the successful ventures.

From Cuba the vessels went to their customary rendez⁄vous in Jamaica, where Governor Modyford was put to some inconvenience to determine how to receive Captain Morgan, whose commission had authorized attacks on ships only. It would appear, however, from his report sent to the Duke of Albemarle, that either the real safety of the colony or the ingenuity of the resourceful Morgan satisfied him that, as Morgan's report showed that both in Cuba and at Puerto Bello preparations had been under way for an expedition against Jamaica, the actions of Cap⁄tain Morgan were justifiable.

Whether less drastic operations by the privateers would have averted or postponed open war with Spain is uncer⁄tain, but in view of the attacks which had successfully been made, reprisals were to be expected, and Governor Modyford enlisted the active co⁄operation of Morgan in following up the advantages already gained. An expedi⁄

tion was planned to the coast of Venezuela with Mara⁄
caibo as the chief objective. In the autumn of 1668,
Morgan arranged to gather together a fleet of privateers
at the Isle le Vache, Hispaniola, and took there with him
ten vessels and some eight hundred men from Jamaica.
He was joined by many other privateers, both English
and French, and by His Majesty's frigate "Oxford"
(thirty⁄four guns) which had been sent at the urgent re⁄
quest of Modyford, to the end that the expedition should
not only have its legitimacy made more certain, but that
some effective restraint should be exercised over the some⁄
what unruly privateers.

On the second of January, 1669, a council of war was
held and plans arranged both as to intercepting an ex⁄
pected Spanish fleet and for a proposed attack upon Car⁄
tagena. At a dinner of the commanders on board the
"Oxford," following the council, an explosion occurred,
wrecking the ship. A number of the officers and two
hundred or more men were lost, included among whom
were some of the crew of a French vessel, held as prison⁄
ers under the charge that they had wantonly attacked and
looted an English merchantman.

The French captain, who was not among those lost,
was subsequently convicted of piracy at Jamaica and his
ship, the "Cour Volant" (afterwards renamed the "Satis⁄
"faction"), confiscated. It is evident that Modyford had
some doubt as to the weight of the evidence communi⁄

cated by Morgan, as he granted the French commander a reprieve, but he did not return his ship which subse/ quently became Morgan's flag/ship. The loss incurred by the explosion and certain defections caused Morgan to give up for the moment the more ambitious plan to attack Cartagena and he reverted to his original objective of Maracaibo. In March, with eight vessels and about five hundred men, he bombarded and overcame the forts at the entrance to Lake Maracaibo and entered the town itself without serious opposition. The power to resist on the part of the garrison and inhabitants was greatly les/ sened because less than two years before the place had been sacked by the notorious French buccaneers L'Olon/ nais and le Basque. The description by Exquemelin of the plundering of this place and the treatment of the peo/ ple is not a cheerful tale.

Whatever may have been the provocation, the excesses seem to have been extreme. Much booty was collected and terms of ransom arranged. With certain of the citi/ zens as hostages, Morgan betook himself, men, and ships to an anchorage off the town of Maracaibo and awaited the ransom money. Meantime three large Spanish men/ of/war had arrived off the entrance to the Lake, and by some means the forts at the entrance had been newly manned while Morgan had been pillaging the settlements at the farther end of the Lake. Morgan displayed that courage and quick resourcefulness which always distin/

guished him. Gaining a short respite by entering into correspondence with the Spanish Admiral, he prepared a fire-ship in the guise of a man-of-war. Then without delay he seized the advantage which always in naval war-fare obtains to the attacker and bore down on the Spanish ships. The fire-ship grappled with the flag-ship the "Almirante" (of forty guns), the second of the Spanish ships was forced to run aground where she was fired by her own crew, while the third was captured by Morgan. From the burning "Almirante" he secured some twenty thousand pieces of eight, partially molten by the great heat. With the ransom, amounting to another twenty thousand, and about five hundred head of cattle safely aboard, he cleverly slipped by the forts at the entrance and by the end of May, with his fleet, was safely anchored at Port Royal, Jamaica.

It is not strange that the Spanish Court did not view these events in a friendly spirit, and the Ambassador of Spain in England did not profess satisfaction with the English explanation that the West Indies were excluded from the mutual treaty obligations. For a brief interval operations against the Spanish in the West Indies were suspended, but in the spring of 1669, Spain began active reprisals. For a period the tables were turned. A fleet of six war vessels, several of good size and well armed, came out from Spain with orders which were intended to make effective replies to unsatisfactory explanations given at

London. English merchant ships were plundered. Privateers were commissioned by the Governors of Puerto Bello and other Spanish strongholds. Jamaica was filled with stories of destruction and cruelties. Modyford appears to have been under orders from home to commit no acts of open war and earnestly besought the home Government to give him power to act at his discretion.

The necessity for action was hastened by the landing on the north side of Jamaica, in June, 1670, of a Spanish expedition from Cuba brought thence in two men-of-war from St. Jago de Cuba. The size of the landing-party was too small to do more than a moderate amount of damage and then quickly to leave the island. The torch was literally lighted. Modyford sent for Morgan and gave him a commission as Commander-in-Chief of all ships of war attached to Jamaica and permission to collect all available privateers. His instructions and authority were not limited to the defence of the island, but permitted him to seize and destroy enemy ships and to attack any ports where there existed materials or vessels useful to the enemy for the war. The instructions include permission to Morgan to advise his men, in respect to prospective booty, "that "they shall have all the goods, merchandises, etc. which "may be got in this expedition to be divided amongst them "according to their usual rules." * As it was the expedi-

* In this division the rules required the setting apart of one fifteenth for the King and one tenth for the Admiral, at this time the Duke of York. According to Exquemelin, Morgan received one hundredth part, every Captain the share

tion which Morgan now undertook, more even than those previously commanded by him, which earned for Mor' gan a reputation for piracy, it is well to note these instruc' tions which were to guide him as well as the conditions which led to the orders being given. That the Governor and Council of Jamaica had in mind the necessity for a clear record to justify their action, particularly in view of the moderation urged by the home Government, is shown by the extensive records in the Council Minutes.

The resolution of the Council recites that ". . . the " Queen Regent of Spain did, by her Scedula dated at " Madrid the 20th of April, 1669, command her respec' "tive governors in the Indies to make open war against "the subjects of our Sovereign Lord the King in those " parts, and also that the Governor of St. Jago de Cuba " hath executed the same by granting commissions of war "against us, and lately in a most hostile manner landed " his men in three places of the north side of this island, " marching as far as he durst into the country, burning all " the houses they came at, killing and taking prisoners all "the inhabitants they could meet with ; . . . That divers " of the rest of the Spanish governors have granted com' " missions and are levying forces against us, and have (as " we are credibly informed) made St. Jago of Cuba their " present magazine and their rendezvous, where there re'

of eight men, and extra allotments were made to various persons and as com- pensation for various services and casualties.

"spective forces are to embody and unite for the speedy "invasion of this island. . . ."

The resolution of the Council conveys to the Governor the exceptional authority needed to deal with the situa' tion and then urges him to grant a commission "to Ad' "miral Henry Morgan to be Admiral and Commander'in' "Chief of all the ships of war belonging to this harbour, ". . . and requiring him with all possible speed to draw "them into one fleet, and with them to put to sea for the "security of the coasts . . . and to attack and seize, and "destroy all the enemy's vessels that come within his "reach; and also for destroying the stores and magazines "laid up for this war . . . and that he have power to land "in the enemy's country as many of his men as he shall "judge needful, and with them to march out to such "places as he shall be informed the said magazines and "forces are; . . . and finally to do all manner of exploits "which may tend to the preservation and quiet of this "island, being his Majesty's chief interest in the In' "dies. . . ."

As we know that Morgan had a sense of humour, it seems certain that he must have chuckled over the au' thority "to do all manner of exploits." Certainly no cour' ageous seaman, untrammelled by an over'delicate sense of merciful justice, could have asked for more sweeping authority. Whatever may have been his behaviour and that of those under him on this expedition, it cannot be

maintained that the saving cloak of legality did not en-
velop him, notwithstanding the somewhat half-hearted
moderation given to these instructions later.

On the seventeenth of August, 1670, Morgan sailed
from Jamaica with eleven vessels and six hundred men
for his usual rendezvous at Hispaniola, where in due
course his fleet was augmented until he had under him
some thirty-six ships, all but eight of which were built in
England.

While engaged in getting together, provisioning and
equipping his fleet, Morgan despatched various vessels
to collect information and supplies from the Cuban and
South-American coasts. Meanwhile negotiations were
under way at Madrid and a peace treaty seemed so immi-
nent that Modyford received instructions from England
to direct the privateers to forbear all hostilities on land
against the Spaniards. These instructions had been communicated to Morgan on the eve of his departure from
Jamaica, and it appears to have been understood between
them that, while necessity would compel Morgan to send
men ashore for water and provisions, no attacks would be
made unless he found preparations under way hostile to
the safety of Jamaica.

It is evident that little confidence was felt in Jamaica
in the efficacy of any "scraps of paper" signed at Madrid to protect the island, as Governor Modyford continued to exert himself to help strengthen Morgan's fleet at

Hispaniola, sending him from time to time additional vessels and men. By the first of December, Morgan found his fleet of thirty-six ships manned by some eighteen hundred men in readiness for sailing. At a Council of War it was determined to give up or postpone a contemplated attack on St. Jago de Cuba and that the safety of Jamaica would be best served by taking Panamá, the Governor of which had been particularly active in granting commissions to privateers against the English.

It may be suspected that Morgan's boast to the Governor of Panamá that he would return within the twelve-month may have had some influence on the plans. By the middle of December, Providence Island was taken, guides to the Panamá shore paths obtained, and about the twentieth, three ships with some four hundred and fifty men were sent forward to capture and silence the forts at the entrance to the Chagres River. Word had reached Panamá from Cartagena of the impending attack and the garrisons at the entrance forts had been greatly re-enforced, as had those at Puerto Bello. Exquemelin, who, although possibly unreliable as to details affecting Morgan, was certainly an eye-witness, gives a detailed account of the actions which took place.

The detachment of Morgan's men landed about three miles from the fort or castle of San Lorenzo early in the morning. They were troubled by the open space near the castle which exposed them to fire when in a position which did not enable them to effectively return it. It was necessary, therefore, to risk an immediate assault. At first this was not successful; but through a fortunate accident, according to Exquemelin, the thatched roofs of the houses within the castle walls were set on fire by flaming arrows, and in the consequent confusion they captured the outside palisades and ultimately, the next day, the cas- tle itself. The Governor, who had commanded the de- fence in person, was killed. Both the attack and defence had been conducted with great bravery and the losses were severe. Of over three hundred men within the cas- tle not over thirty were left alive, although a few others were said to have escaped and fled to Panamá with the news of the disaster.

Upon Morgan's arrival with the rest of his fleet a few days after the capture of the castle, he had the misfortune to wreck his flag-ship and several smaller vessels on the bar at the entrance to the Chagres River.

He did not make the mistake made at Maracaibo and leave the fort at the entrance unguarded; but he repaired the castle walls, and left three hundred men to defend it and protect the anchored fleet. With about fourteen hun- dred in a few of the smaller vessels and a fleet of canoes he started forward on the ninth of January, 1671, to attack Panamá. After travelling one day and a portion of another by the river, they were forced by low water to leave their boats. About one hundred and seventy-five men were left

to guard the boats, and on the third day they began a difficult march overland with assistance rendered by some of
the smaller canoes. On the fourth day they found an
abandoned ambuscade of the Spaniards, who either through
knowledge that they were outnumbered or in a panic had
retreated without offering resistance. Morgan had de-
pended upon the country for sustenance and found that
the Spaniards had been careful to leave no provisions behind them; he was consequently hard put to find food for
his men. On the fifth day they encountered another
freshly abandoned ambuscade, but no provisions. The
men, worn out with the hard marches through tropical
forests, were indeed reduced to extremity; but for the fortunate discovery of a small quantity of meal and grain in
sacks hidden in a cave or grotto, together with a quantity of wine and plantains, the expedition might have been
wiped out by hunger and the illnesses certain to follow
exposure to the tropical climate while in a weakened condition. Somewhat strengthened by the food, they continued their march on the sixth day and happily found a barn
full of maize. The report of Morgan and the account by
Exquemelin differ as to the exact day on which the
events of this weary march took place, but agree as to the
chief incidents.

The suffering was great; but in spite of murmurings
Morgan seems to have kept his men well in hand. On the
seventh day, with their supply of maize exhausted and

their stomachs empty, they were cheered by the sight of a village with many wreaths of curling smoke indicating the preparation of food. With a rush the place was invaded. It was empty of both people and provisions and the smoke was caused by the thatched houses themselves which had been set alight by the fleeing Spaniards and Indians. At this village, about eight Spanish leagues from Panamá, the small canoes, which up to this point had been of help particularly to those weakened by hunger or illness, had to be abandoned, with a small company who were directed to take them back to the place where the boats had been left under guard. On the eighth day Morgan sent a reconnoitring body of two hundred men to search out the best path to Panamá. This body, while passing through a place called Quebrada Obscura, were suddenly the target for thousands of arrows, shot apparently from invisible crevices in a neighbouring mountainside. Notwithstanding their attempted defence and the quick flight of the Indians who had made up the attacking force, the Captain of the party and a substantial number of his men were killed.

That night a heavy rain came, and Morgan found it necessary to push forward not only because of the need for food, but to get shelter where his ammunition could be kept dry. On the ninth day things looked brighter. The ocean was in sight and they could distinguish vessels and islands off the shore. They came into a valley well stocked with cattle, and building fires they rested and feasted upon the flesh which in their hunger and haste was scarcely cooked. With a smaller body in front to do scout duty, Morgan pressed on. Before night the steeple of a church in Panamá could be seen. A reconnoitring party of horse/ men from the city viewed their camp that night and an unsuccessful attempt was made to reach the camp by shots from the largest guns within the city. Early on the tenth day, Morgan began his march for the city, not by the direct road, but through an irksome and roundabout way, through which he was led by one of his competent guides. An approach from the direction taken was not expected by the Spanish, their batteries were not in po/ sition for effective use, and they were forced to come out and meet Morgan with a force consisting of two squad/ rons, four regiments of foot, and a large number of wild bulls driven by Indians and negroes. It was indeed a for/ midable force for Morgan's worn/out men to encounter, and Exquemelin confesses that but for the fact that no quarter could be expected and no way of escape was open, many of the men that day would have lacked the cour/ age to fight at all. As it was they had to fight resolutely or die.

After two hours of severe fighting, with great bravery shown on each side, the victory was with Morgan, and the remnants of the Spanish body fled back into the city. Morgan's men were too harassed and wearied with their fighting and days of marching to immediately follow up the advantage gained.

From prisoners taken Morgan learned the strength of the Spanish forces, which were reported to amount in all to four hundred horse, twenty-four companies of foot. and two thousand wild bulls (upon which great dependence was placed to make havoc when caused to run through the English camp).

The various reports of the actual number of Spaniards engaged in the defence of the city are conflicting. Morgan in his report states the numbers to have been twenty-one hundred foot and six hundred horse. The report sent to Spain by the President of Panamá gives the numbers as fourteen hundred negroes, Indians and slaves, all, according to his report, badly armed; his report also states that his artillery consisted of wooden guns covered with hides.

Morgan and Exquemelin both state that there were several raised batteries with many guns, and that at the point where the highway entered the city the Spaniards had erected a fort and mounted eight brass guns of large size. Morgan even specifies the exact number of brass guns used in the various defences to have been thirty-two. There are four detailed accounts of the taking of the city: Morgan's report, the account of Exquemelin, the account of one William Frogge (one of Morgan's men), and the report of the President of Panamá. A comparison

VIEW OF PANAMA
From an old Dutch print

and analysis of these reports leads to the conviction that in the main the account of Exquemelin is true, although it is not strange if both his account and the report of Morgan somewhat over-stated the strength of the Span-ish forces.

The actual taking of the town is described by Ex-quemelin as follows:

" Captain Morgan having heard this Information, [i.e., "the fact that a fort with brass guns protected the prin-"cipal entrance] gave Orders instantly they should march "another way. But before setting forth, he made a Review " of all his Men, whereof he found both killed and wounded "a considerable number, and much greater than had been "believed. Of the Spaniards were found 600 dead upon "the place, besides the wounded, and Prisoners. The " Pirats were nothing discouraged, seeing their number "so much diminished, but rather filled with greater Pride "than before, perceiving what huge Advantage they had "obtained against their Enemies. Thus having rested "themselves some while, they prepared to march cour-"agiously towards the City, plighting their Oaths to one "another in general, they would fight till never a Man "were left alive. With this Courage they recommenc'd "their March, either to conquer, or be conquered, carry-"ing with them all the Prisoners.

" They found much difficulty in their Approach unto "the City. For within the Town the Spaniards had placed

"many great Guns, at several Quarters thereof, some of
"which were charged with small pieces of Iron, and oth-
"ers with Musket-Bullets: With all these they saluted the
"Pirats, at their drawing nigh unto the place, and gave
"them full and frequent Broad-sides, firing at them in-
"cessantly. From whence it came to pass, that unavoid-
"ably they lost at every step they advanced, great num-
"bers of Men. But neither these manifest Dangers of their
"Lives, nor the sight of so many of their own, as dropped
"down continually at their Sides, could deter them from
"advancing farther, and gaining Ground every moment
"upon the Enemy. Thus although the Spaniards never
"ceased to fire, and act the best they could for their De-
"fence, yet notwithstanding they were forced to deliver
"the City after the space of three hours Combat. And
"the Pirats having now possessed themselves thereof, both
"killed and destroyed as many, as attempted to make the
"least Opposition against them. The Inhabitants had caused
"the best of their Goods to be transported unto more
"remote and occult places. Howbeit they found within
"the City as yet, several Ware-houses, very well stockt
"with all sorts of Merchandize, as well Silks and Cloths,
"as Linnen, and other things of considerable value. As
"soon as the first Fury of their entrance into the City was
"over, Captain Morgan assembled all his Men at a certain
"place which he assigned, and there commanded them
"under very great penalties, that none of them should

"dare to drink or taste any Wine. The Reason he gave for
"this Injunction, was, because he had received private
"Intelligence, that it had been all poysoned by the Span-
"iards. Howbeit it was the Opinion of many, he gave
"these prudent Orders, to prevent the Debauchery of his
"People, which he foresaw would be very great at the
"beginning, after so much Hunger sustained by the way.
"Fearing withal, least the Spaniards seeing them in Wine,
"should rally their Forces, and fall upon the City, and use
"them as inhumanely as they had used the Inhabitants
"before.

"Captain Morgan, as soon as he had placed Guards
"at several Quarters, where he thought necessary, both
"within and without the City of Panama, immediately
"commanded 25 Men to seize a great Boat, which had
"stuck in the Mud of the Port, for want of Water at a low
"Tide, so that she could not put out to Sea. The same
"day, about Noon, he caused certain Men privately to set
"Fire unto several great Edifices of the City, no body
"knowing from whence the Fire proceeded, nor who
"were the Authors thereof, much less what Motives per-
"swaded Captain Morgan thereunto, which are as yet
"unknown to this day. The Fire increased so fast, that
"before Night the greatest part of the City was in a
"Flame.* Captain Morgan endeavor'd to make the Pub-

* Exquemelin is probably in error. The Spanish records state that the Spaniards set the fires apparently by direction of the President of Panamá to prevent
Morgan seizing and carrying off the goods in warehouses, and to otherwise em-
barrass him. Frogge's account substantiates this.

"lick believe, the Spaniards had been the cause thereof,
"which Suspicions he surmised among his own People,
"perceiving they reflected upon him for that Action.
"Many of the Spaniards, as also some of the Pirats, used
"all the means possible, either to extinguish the Flame,
"or by blowing up of Houses with Gun-powder, and pull-
"ing down others to stop its progress. But all was in vain;
"for in less than half an hour it consumed a whole Street.
"All the Houses of this City were built with Cedar, be-
"ing of very curious and magnificent Structure, and richly
"adorned within. Especially with Hangings and Paint-
"ings, where of part were already transported out of the
"Pirats way, and another great part were consumed by
"the Voracity of the Fire.

"There belonged unto this City (which is also the
"Head of a Bishoprick) eight Monasteries, whereof seven
"were for Men, and one for Women; two stately
"Churches, and one Hospital. The Churches and Monas-
"teries were all richly adorned with Altar-pieces and
"Paintings, huge quantity of Gold and Silver, with other
"precious things; all which the Ecclesiasticks had hidden
"and concealed. Besides which Ornaments, here were
"to be seen 2000 Houses, of magnificent and prodigious
"Building, as being all, or the greatest part, inhabited by
"Merchants of that Countrey, who are vastly rich. For
"the rest of the Inhabitants, of lesser quality, and Trades-
"men, this City contained 5000 Houses more. Here were

"also great number of Stables, which served for the
"Horses and Mules that carry all the Plate, belonging as
"well unto the King of Spain, as private Men, towards
"the Coast of the North-Sea. The neighboring Fields be-
"longing to this City, are all cultivated with fertil Planta-
"tions and pleasant Gardens, which afford delicious Pros-
"pects unto the Inhabitants the whole year long.

"The Genoeses had in this City of Panama a stately
"and magnificent House, belonging to their Trade and
"Commerce of Negro's. This Building likewise was com-
"manded by Captain Morgan to be set on Fire; whereby
"it was burnt to the very Ground. Besides which pile of
"Building, there were consumed to the number of 200
"Ware-houses, and great number of Slaves, who had hid
"themselves therein, together with an infinite multitude
"of Sacks of Meal. The Fire of all which Houses and
"Buildings, was seen to continue four Weeks after the
"day it began.

"The Pirats i' th' mean while, at least the greatest part
"of them, incamped some time without the City, fearing
"and expecting that the Spaniards would come and fight
"them anew. For it was known, they had an incompar-
"able number of Men more than the Pirats were. This
"occasion'd them to keep the Field, thereby to preserve
"their Forces united, which now were very much dimin-
"ished, by the losses of the precedent Battels. As also be-
"cause they had a great many wounded, all which they

" had put into one of the Churches which alone remained
"standing, the rest being consumed by the Fire. More
" over, beside these Decreases of their Men, Captain Mor
"gan had sent a Convoy of 150 Men unto the Castle of
"Chagre, to carry the News of his Victory obtained
"against Panama.

" They saw many times whole Troops of Spaniards
"cruize to and fro in the Campaign Fields, which gave
"them occasion to suspect their rallying anew. Yet they
"never had the courage to attempt any thing against the
"Pirats. I'th' afternoon of this fatal day, Captain Morgan
"reentred again the City with his Troops, to the in
"tent every one might take up their Lodgings, which
"now they could hardly find, very few Houses having
"escaped the Desolation of the Fire. Soon after they fell
"to seeking very carefully among the Ruines and Ashes,
"for Utensils of Plate, or Gold, which peradventure were
"not quite wasted by the Flames. And of such things
"they found no small number in several places. Especially
"in Wells and Cisterns, where the Spaniards had hid them
"from the covetous search of the Pirats.

" The next day Captain Morgan dispatcht away two
"Troops of Pirats, of 150 Men each, being all very stout
"Souldiers, and well armed, with Orders to seek for the
"Inhabitants of Panama, who were escaped from the
"hands of their Enemies. These Men, having made sev
"eral Excursions up and down the Campaign Fields,

"Woods and Mountains adjoyning to Panama, returned
"after two days time, bringing with them above 200 Pris-
"oners, between Men, Women, and Slaves. The same day
"returned also the Boat above-mentioned, which Captain
"Morgan had sent into the South-Sea, bringing with her
"three other Boats, which they had taken in a little while.
"But all these Prizes they could willingly have given,
"yea although they had imployed greater labor into the
"bargain, for one certain Galeon which miraculously
"escaped their Industry, being very richly laden with all
"the King's Plate, and great quantity of Riches of Gold,
"Pearl, Jewels, and other most precious Goods, of all the
"best and richest Merchants of Panama. On board of this
"Galeon were also the religious Women belonging to
"the Nunnery of the said City, who had imbarked with
"them, all the Ornaments of their Church, consisting in
"great quantity of Gold, Plate, and other things of great
"value."

Morgan would have liked to send boats after this galleon, but his men were given up to debaucheries that
they "chose rather to satiate their lust and appetite . . .
"than to lay hold on the occasion of such an huge advan-
"tage." Various boats were, however, captured, which,
although of less value than the galleon, were well laden
with merchandise, and on one of them were found twenty
thousand pieces of eight. Morgan was encouraged to remain longer than he had intended at Panamá by the news

that the detachment which he had left at Chagres had made several valuable captures in the adjacent waters, in-cluding one Spanish ship with a cargo of provisions.

By prolonging his stay Morgan was able to search the surrounding country, finding many hiding-places and de-posits of valuables until he had gathered a great quantity of plunder. The cruelties inflicted on the harassed Span-iards during the vigorous search that was made are viv-idly described by Exquemelin and denied by Morgan.

The following extract from Exquemelin's account, it is to be hoped, is not accurate or at the worst is excep-tional:

"Captain Morgan used to send forth daily parties of "200 Men, to make In-roads into all the Fields and Coun-"trey thereabouts, and when one party came back, an-"other consisting of 200 more was ready to go forth. By "this means they gathered in a short time huge quantity "of Riches, and no lesser number of prisoners. These being "brought into the City, were presently put unto the most "exquisite Tortures imaginable, to make them confess "both other peoples Goods and their own. Here it hap-"pened, that one poor and miserable Wretch, was found "in the House of a Gentleman of great Quality, who had "put on, amidst that confusion of things, a pair of Taf-"fety Breeches, belonging to his Master, with a little "silver Key hanging at the Strings thereof. This being "perceived by the Pirats, they immediately asked him,

"Where was the Cabinet of the said Key? His Answer
"was, He knew not what was become of it, but only that
"finding those Breeches in his Master's House, he had
"made bold to wear them. Not being able to extort any
"other Confession out of him, they first put him upon
"the Rack, wherewith they inhumanely dis-joynted his
"Arms. After this, they twisted a Cord about his Fore-
"head, which they wrung so hard, that his Eyes appeared
"as big as Eggs, and were ready to fall out of his Skull.
"But neither with these Torments, could they obtain any
"positive Answer to their Demands. Whereupon they
"soon after hung him up by the Testicles, giving him
"infinite Blows and Stripes, mean while he was under
"that intolerable pain and posture of Body. Afterwards
"they cut off his Nose and Ears, and singed his Face with
"burning Straw, till he could speak nor lament his Misery
"no longer. Then loosing all Hopes of hearing any Con-
"fession from his Mouth, they commanded a Negro to run
"him through with a Lance, which put an end to his Life,
"and a period to their cruel and inhumane Tortures. After
"this execrable manner, did many others of those miser-
"able Prisoners finish their days, the common Sport and
"Recreation of these Pirats, being these, and other Trag-
"edies not inferiour to these.

"They spared, in these their Cruelties, no Sex, nor
"Condition whatsoever. For as to religious Persons and
"Priests, they granted them less Quarter than unto others,

"unless they could produce a considerable Sum of Money,
"capable of being a sufficient Ransom. Women them⁄
"selves were no better used, except they would condescend
"unto the libidinous Demands and Concupiscency of the
"Pirats. For such as would not consent unto their Lust,
"were treated with all the Rigour and Cruelty imaginable.
"Captain Morgan, their Leader and Commander, gave
"them no good Example in this point. For as soon as any
"beautiful Woman was brought as a Prisoner to his pres⁄
"ence, he used all the means he could possible, both of
"Rigor and Mildness, to bend them to his lascivious will
"and pleasure."

After remaining at Panamá the space of three weeks,
Morgan had various pack animals collected on which were
loaded the considerable booty which had been gathered.
Through a timely warning Morgan at this time prevented
the desertion of a portion of his men, who had planned
to escape with a goodly part of the riches in some of the
captured vessels in the harbour. Shortly after the middle
of February, 1671, Morgan left the ruined city with nearly
two hundred pack animals loaded with silver, gold, goods
of all sorts, and food for the trip, together with a large
number of prisoners. These prisoners he threatened to take
to Jamaica unless ransomed by their friends, and from a
stopping⁄place on the road to where he had left his boats
and canoes he did a profitable trade in exchanging prisoners
for substantial payments. On the march back to Chagres

an effective rear guard was under the command of Colonel Blendry Morgan, a kinsman of the Admiral.

After the arrival at Chagres, division of the spoils was
made, not without a great amount of quarrelling as was to
be expected, and early in March, 1671, after demolishing
the fort, Morgan set sail for Port Royal. Exquemelin
accuses him of having sailed secretly with only three or
four vessels, and states that by the end of August not more
than ten of the original thirty-six vessels had made their
way back to Jamaica.

It does not seem probable that Exquemelin was in a
position to know accurately these details, and it is probable that the absences and delays of the ships were for the
most part voluntary on the part of their crews, who it is
to be assumed preferred the free range of the Caribbean
to the control to which they would be subjected at
Jamaica.

The Council of Jamaica on the thirty-first of May,
1671, gave a vote of thanks to Morgan in a form which
expressed approval of his accomplishment. More than
vague rumours of discontent with his division of the
spoils kept coming in, however, as the scattered vessels
of his fleet came into port. It is difficult to believe that
Morgan was free from blame in this respect. It seems
more probable that the free-and-easy habits of his life had
made him not too scrupulous in a division which so intimately touched his own interests.

In July, 1670, at Madrid a treaty between England and Spain had been concluded for "restraining depredations "and establishing peace" in the New World.

Although the plea of Modyford, that the commission to Morgan had been given in good faith to avert a real danger to Jamaica, was probably to a large extent true, and undoubtedly secretly winked at by the officers of the Government, yet a scapegoat was needed. Modyford was summoned home a prisoner. In April, 1672, Morgan was obliged to follow, a prisoner in the "Welcome" frigate. Admiral Morgan had, however, accomplished too much and had too great a popularity to remain long in disgrace. Influential friends cleared him, so that within little more than a year he was appointed Deputy Governor of Jamaica (the Earl of Carlisle had been named Governor), but he did not take his post until late in 1674 after Lord Vaughan had been appointed Governor of the island and Morgan Lieutenant Governor. In November of that year, Morgan was knighted. Morgan arrived in Jamaica before Lord Vaughan and with authority of the Council acted as Governor for a few days before the arrival of Vaughan.

The seventeenth century was not a period when nations were over particular as to methods, and it is to be remembered that the incessant struggle in the West Indies meant more to the European countries involved than the single question of booty gained and private fortunes made. Morgan almost invariably secured his objective. His name alone was a terror to the enemies of England. Excesses were certainly committed in his name; whether by him personally or not is less certain. There is much contem/ porary evidence that Morgan was not so black as he was painted by his detractors.

In 1672, the Commander of the forces in Jamaica, Major/General Banister, wrote to Lord Arlington, "he " [Morgan] is a well deserving person, and one of great " courage and conduct, who may, with his Majesty's pleas/ " ure, perform good public service at home or be very ad/ " vantageous to this island if war should again break forth "with the Spaniards."

To what extent the apology printed by William Crooke, publisher, was dictated by expediency and to what extent by conviction is not known, but it is an interesting docu/ ment which can appropriately be submitted as evidence in Morgan's favour. With unimportant omissions it is as follows: *

"The History of the Bucaniers of America, having "been written in the Dutch Language, by John Esque/ "meling, and afterwards translated into the Spanish by " Alonso de Bonne Maison, Dr. of Physick, was lately done "out of Spanish into English, and thereupon unadvisedly "printed, as appearing then unto me to be only a general "history of Action performed by several Persons, at sev/

* The page references are to Crooke's Second edition of Exquemelin's *His-tory of the Bucaniers.*

"eral times, and likewise in several Places. How so it is,
"that amongst divers other Actions there rehearsed, are
"also contained the unparallell′d Exploits of that Valiant
"and Heroick Gentleman, Sir Henry Morgan; upon
"which no reflection was then made. But, since the pub′
"lication of the said History (which was done by me in
"a trading way, and with no other design) I have been
"credibly informed by certain gentlemen, who belong
"unto the acquaintance of Sir Henry, that several things
"are therein delivered, the which are both falsely reported
"by John Esquemeling, and wrongfully represented, and
"consequently are much redounding to the Disreputation
"and Dishonour of that Worthy Person, Sir Hen. Mor′
"gan; For the Wounds of whose Reputation by that Au′
"thor, I have been, ever since my better information, both
"heartily sorrowful, and concerned in the sincerity of my
"mind; and in testimony thereof, have thought it con′
"venient, by these times, humbly to solicit, and desire
"the pardon of that noble and generous Spirit, for as much
"as by me hath been contributed thereunto, by printing
"the English Translation.

   "The Sincerity of the whole case was this: That the
"truth of the particulars contained in the History of John
"Esquemeling, were not, at the publishing thereof, nei′
"ther could they possibly by me be known, as being to′
"tally unacquainted with those Affairs, or with the Per′
"son or Merits, of Sir Henry Morgan. Yea tho′ I made

"divers Enquiries thereunto, I could not be so happy
"as to learn, whether that worthy Person were, as yet,
"among the living or not; as I conceive I may be able
"to convince, both by sufficient and undubitable wit-
"nesses. Hereupon, the Book was, by me, taken as a
"general History, which has been already seen in several
"Languages abroad, and, for as much as a great part
"thereof contained the Heroic Actions of our English
"Nation it was accordingly printed by a strict Transla-
"tion from the Spanish. But, whatever points in the said
"History, either do misrepresent the heroic Actions of
"that worthy Gentleman, or do in any wise, reflect upon
"his Honour, I do hereby declare, and sincerely, in the
"presence of God Almighty, protest, that I never had in
"mind, the least intention or design, either of reflecting,
"or aspersing of him, or any other Person whatsoever,
"named in that History. And, as aforesaid I am both
"heartily sorry, and not a little perplex'd to understand
"that Sir Henry Morgan should receive any, the least
"offense at that, which was not in the least by me intended
"in the said English Translation.

   "The integrity of my Intention, and the whole truth
"of my Proceedings, being thus declared; Yet, notwith-
"standing, for the greater satisfaction of the Publick, and
"to evince more clearly the Sincerity thereof, I do hereby
"again and again, humbly beg the Pardon of Sir Henry,
"if anything I have done, by publishing that Book, hath

"given any just occasion of offense unto Him, or been
"the least cause of diminishing the Splendour and Worth
"of his Deserts. Yea, to be a little more free in this Ac⁄
"knowledgement, I do hereby own my unadvisedness in
"giving to a Spanish Translation. (But at that time there
"was no License appointed for the review of Books) in a
"matter that so nearly concerned that Nation; and where⁄
"in Justice could not easily be done unto Sir Henry, in
"the Relation, without reflecting either on the Courage
"or Conduct of the Spaniards in those Parts: For which
"unadvisedness of my own, I do, once more, pray his
"Pardon; and shall confess it an Act of high Generosity
"and Goodness in him, to accept of this my Acknowledge⁄
"ment, instead of putting me into the trouble of a ver⁄
"dict at Common Law; altho nothing was ever more re⁄
"mote from my Thoughts, as the designing, or intending
"him the said Sir Henry Morgan, the least Prejudice or
"Scandal.

"From hence, to do all the Justice and Equity that I
"possibly can, unto the Merits of Sir Henry, according to
"what I heretofore, so spontaneously promised in the Pref⁄
"ace unto the second Volume of the History of the
"Bucaniers I shall now proceed to correct such Passages
"of the History, as, according to the Notice I have re⁄
"ceived of Faults. The which Passages for the better
"Credit thereof, I do Acknowledge to have obtained from
"some worthy Persons his Friends, who were Witnesses,

"as I have, unto the whole Transactions there related, and
"from whom I got this Information, and how to Correct
"them as follows:

"Page 32. Here the Author, John Esquemeling, hath
"mistaken the Origin of Sir Henry Morgan, for he was
"a Gentleman's Son of good Quality, in the County of
"Monmouth, and was never a Servant unto anybody in
"his life, unless unto his Majesty, the late King of Eng-
"land. Neither did he ever sail, but by Commission of
"the Governor of those Parts.

"The Cruelties and barbarous Usages of the Spaniards,
"when at his Mercy, or his Prisoners, do manifestly Re-
"flect on the Reputation of Sir Henry Morgan, and were
"wholly an error in the Original Author of this History.
"As, for Instance, in Pages 44, 49, 61, 64, 65, 25, 30,
"31, &c, the Cruelties there related, after the taking of
"Puerto del Principe, and the blowing up the Castle at
"Puerto Velo, are not true. For the castle was left stand-
"ing, and quarter was given unto all that yielded. And,
"moreover Sir Henry Morgan, having power, by his
"Commission, both of Life and Limb, over all his fleet
"and Army, it is not credible that he would suffer either
"any such Cruelties or Debaucheries to be done. Neither
"(as I am told) was there any such Cruelty committed,
"as the Wrecking of a Fool or the Torturing of a Rich
"Portugezen, or the causing a Negro to kill several Span-
"ish Prisoners thereby to create an hatred of the Span-

"iards against him and with intent to prevent his return-
"ing unto them. Or, the hanging up any Persons by the
"Testicles. No more Truth was there in that Story, that
"many Religious were pistolled; for, no such Persons
"were killed, unless they were found in Arms.

"In Page 54, the Author hath also mistaken Admiral
"Morgan's sailing from Puerto Velo. For, instead of go-
"ing to Cuba, as is there related, the Fleet sailed directly
"to Jamaica. In the succeeding Page likewise, the Ship,
"there said to come from New England, was the Oxford
"Frigat. And the French Ship there mentioned was a
"French Pirat, who had lately plundered a Vessel from
"New England, and upon the Complaint made unto the
"Governour of Jamaica, he sent the Frigat out to take
"her, which was accordingly done; and the Frigat after-
"wards joyned with the Fleet of Admiral Morgan, by the
"Command and Orders of his Majesty's said then Gov-
"ernour of Jamaica. There was, likewise, no Advice given
"to Admiral Morgan about Fireship mentioned Page 70;
"but rather, it was entirely his own contrivance. Also,
"the style of the Letter of the Spanish Admiral unto him,
"is wrong; for he styled him, Captain Morgan, Head of
"the English Fleet, and not Commander of the Pirate.
"In like manner, timely orders were given by Sir Henry
"Morgan for taking the Galeon mention'd in page 29,
"but were neglected by such as received the Orders.

"The Expedition performed by Admiral Morgan

"against Panama, was not undertaken without Commis-
" sion from the then Governour of Jamaica. And it was
"upon the account of new Acts of Hostility, and fresh
" Abuses that had been committed by the Spaniards, upon
"the King of England's subjects of Jamaica; as by the
" Council Minute may sufficiently appear, to any that de-
" sire full satisfaction herein ; and also by the said Com-
" mission, which they may see here inserted."

The records of the complaint of Morgan against
Thomas Malthus (Court of King's Bench, James II, 1685),
who, as previously noted, also published Exquemelin's
" History of the Bucaniers," are additional evidence to
the thoroughness with which Morgan pursued his detractors and may be taken as some further testimony to
the fact that the charges against him were at best exag-
gerated. John Greene, Morgan's attorney, recites in the
complaint " That the Morgan family had always held due
"and natural allegiance to the King, were both by sea
"and land of good fame, and that against all evil deeds,
"piracies, etc., had the greatest abhorrence and disgust,
"and that in the West Indies there are such thieves and
"pirates, called 'buccaneers,' who subsist by piracy, dep-
"redation and evil deeds of all kinds without lawful au-
"thority, that of these people Henry Morgan always had
"and still has hatred; but notwithstanding this, Thomas
"Malthus, not unacquainted with these facts, has cun-
"ningly contrived to injure Henry Morgan's good name

"and fame by printing, spreading abroad and publishing
"a certain false, malicious, scandalous and famous libel
"entitled A History of the Bucaniers."

The specific libels were enumerated and substantial
damages claimed. A jury awarded Morgan two hundred
pounds and costs. There is good reason to assume that the
smallness of the judgment rendered in Morgan's favour
was due to adjustments made outside of the Court, not
perhaps in cash, but in a way to reinstate Morgan in the
good opinion of the people. The second edition of Exquemelin's book published by William Crooke contains
an addition to the preface disclaiming in considerable
measure the responsibility on the part of the publisher to
the words of the author, admitting some errors, but on
the whole a very incomplete apology and rather a defence
of himself as publisher, with some extravagant, if slightly
ironical, expression of laudation of Sir Henry Morgan.
That this was followed later by the sweeping and detailed
public apology which has been quoted here was apparently due to or was a part of the Malthus settlement.

In the "Correspondence of the Family of Hatton,
"A.D. 1601–1704," published by the Camden Society,
1878, is an interesting letter dated twenty-ninth of May,
1697, written by Charles Hatton to Lord Hatton.*

---

* Mr. Frank Cundall, of the Jamaica Institute, was kind enough to call attention to this correspondence, to furnish information about the Pölnitz family,
and to give details as to Morgan's death.

"... shall now give you ye account I then intended
"about Ringrose his relation of Sharps voyage into y^e
"South Sea, wch is called ye 2^d part of ye History of
"ye Buccaneers. About ye yeare 1680 ther came out a
"history of ye Buccaneers, printed in Flanders, in Span,
"ish, pretended to be a translation from Dutch writ by
"one Esquemeling, a Dutch buccaneer, wch Crooke
"a bookseller got translated into English and printed,
"in wch Sr Henry Morgan was represented as a very
"barbarous pyrate. Sr Harry brought his action ag^t
"Crooke, proved all he did was by virtue of a commis,
"sion of ye Governor of Jamaica and ye Kings authority,
"and recovered 300" or 400" damage from Crooke, about
"y^t some I am sure Crook himself told me. After w^{ch},
"his History of ye Buccaneers wase looked upon as fab,
"ulous and sold for noe more than wast paper. But S^r
"Harry Morgan being return'd to Jamaica, and Sharp
"and his comrades their voyage into ye South Sea making
"a great noise, and Sharps journal being printed and sell,
"ing very well, Crooke agrees wth Ringrose, who had
"been a buccaneer wth Sharp, for a relation he had of
"ye exploits done in ye South Sea by Sharp and other
"pyrats; and, to make some recompense to Sr Henry
"Morgan, he was mentioned very honorably and Ring,
"rose his booke stiled ye 2^d part of ye History of Bucca,
"neers, and is generally sold wth ye first, they being both
"printed in 4to.

"The first part of ye History of ye Buccaneers wase
"put forth in French wth some variations and aditions,
"pretended to have been write in Dutch by one Oxeme-
"lin.

"Sr John Narborough's Voyage was about five years
"agoe, as I thinke, printed for Smith and Watford, in an
"8° volume, together wth Martins voyage to Spitsbergen
"and other voyages, wch have sold very well, as also an-
"other booke of voyages by Ran Wolfius and others.

"Dampier is sensible of many mistakes he hath made,
"and in his next volume he will correct them; wch he
"very honestly wou'd not doe in ye 2^d ed. of his first vol-
"ume, for y^t wou'd have been to ye prejudice of all who
"had bought his first volume."

Whilst much that Exquemelin states to Morgan's dis-
credit is undoubtedly coloured by prejudice, it must be
admitted that Morgan did not always so conduct himself
on shore as to completely give the lie to his critics. Even
the dignity of his titles, Admiral, Knight, and Lieutenant-Governor, were not enough to prevent the occasional
out-cropping of his swashbuckler temperament. A reg-
ulated life on shore must have been irksome to him. In
May, 1674, the Assembly voted six hundred pounds special salary to him to be paid during his Lieutenant-Gov-
ernorship. With time on his hands and money in his
pocket, Morgan, according to the reports sent home by
Governor Vaughan, frequented the taverns of Port Royal

drinking and gambling in unseemly fashion. Later in
May, 1676, Vaughan accused him of giving aid to illegal
privateers and of otherwise obstructing the efforts of the
Governor to stop this form of illegal sea commerce. Finally Vaughan made definite charges against both Morgan
and Robert Byndloss (a connection of Morgan through
his wife), both of whom were members of the Council.
Morgan and Byndloss were cited to appear before the
Council in July, 1676, and the examination of the charges
took place before the Governor and eight other members.
A reading of the Minutes in the Council Book of Jamaica
covering the period of this examination, which took in
effect the form of a trial, shows that Morgan had the same
active and resourceful mind in defending himself with
arguments, not always convincing, which he had in actual warfare. Morgan's popularity seems to have been
proof against attacks, as nothing seems to have come
from the proceedings, a full record of which was sent to
England.

From an interesting correspondence at the Public Records Office, London, and in the Journal of the Lords of
Trade and Plantations, it is clear that efforts were made
to persuade both Morgan and Vaughan to patch up their
quarrel.

That Morgan did not wholly lose the confidence of
those in England charged with the administration of the
colony is shown by the fact that under date of thirteenth

of January, 1678, in the Journal of the Lords of Trade
and Plantations a commission is granted to Sir Henry
Morgan, Lieutenant-Governor of Jamaica, to be Captain
of a company of one hundred men. On the same date
Lord Carlisle was appointed Governor of Jamaica to
succeed Vaughan.

For nearly four months, the period between the departure of Vaughan and the arrival of Carlisle, Morgan
again acted as Governor of the island. During Carlisle's
brief term of office the two men appear to have had
friendly relations. Carlisle writes home in a somewhat
kindly way of Morgan's "generous manner" and inti-
mates that whatever allowances are made to him "he will
"be a beggar." For a period after Carlisle went home in
May, 1680, Morgan once again acted as Governor, and
it was during this period that he wrote home despatches
which must have been strange reading to those who knew
well his earlier career.

On the fifth of July, 1680, he writes to Lord Sunder-
land telling of the annoyance along the coast from both
French privateers and those which belong to the island
itself. He urges that "some nimble small frigates for coast-
"ing around the island be supplied," and points out that
nothing can be more fatal to the prosperity of the colony
than the temptingly alluring boldness and success of the
privateers which draw off white servants and all men of
unfortunate or desperate condition. Morgan appears to

have taken particular satisfaction in reporting that he had captured at Bull Bay a notorious privateer.

Among other reports from Morgan to the Lords of Trade and Plantations is one bearing on a certain petition of one Francis Mingham which has interest because it contains a letter from Morgan which throws some light on his own estimate of himself. A portion of the letter follows:

"I left school too young to be a great proficient in "either that or other laws, and have been much more "used to the pike than the book; and as for the profit "there is no porter in this town but can get more money "in the time than I got by this trial. But I was truly put "in to maintain the honor of the court for his Majesty's "service. Without this the act of navigation cannot be "enforced for it is hard to find unbiased juries in the "plantations for such cases. For instance, a ship from Ire- "land came here with several casks of Irish soap, and was "seized by his Majesty's receiver. The case was tried in "the Court of Common Pleas, and the jury found for the "defendant with costs. One witness swore that soap was "vittles and that one might live upon it for a month, "which the jury readily believed and found the aforesaid "verdict. I beg your Lordships to believe that if I have "erred at all in this matter it has been of judgment only. "May God love me no longer than I love justice."

In May, 1681, Sir Thomas Lynch was appointed Governor, and shortly afterwards Morgan's commission as Lieutenant-Governor was rescinded. The appointment of Lynch, on account of previous relations of the two men, was a direct blow at Morgan and things did not go well between them. Morgan technically retained his seat on the Council, but appears to have behaved very intemperately. It is evident Morgan wanted to force out Lynch and to succeed to the post. Lynch seems to have been equally determined to humiliate Morgan, whose temper was not of the best. The Minutes of the Council even record such a frivolous charge as that Morgan had been overheard to say, "God damn the Assembly." Finally Morgan was dismissed from the Council.

For some time Morgan appears to have had his hands full in defending his reputation, as it was during the trying years which now came to him that Exquemelin's book was published in England and the libel suit, already recorded, was prosecuted. Morgan appears, however, to have been determined to remain in Jamaica and re-establish his reputation and position there. In December, 1687, the whole Council recommended the re-admission of Sir Henry Morgan to membership, a request the granting of which was urged upon the King by the Duke of Albemarle. On the twenty-seventh of April, 1688, the King in Council ordered the suspension removed and Morgan was reinstated. Morgan did not, however, live long to enjoy his restored honours. On the twenty-fifth of August,

1688, he died. The ceremonies which marked his death were befitting the great seaman that he was. The following is an extract from the Journal of Captain Lawrence Wright, Commander of His Majesty's ship, "Assistance":

"August 1688.

"Saturday 25 "This day about eleven hours noone "Sir Henry Morgan died, & the 26th was brought over "from Passage/fort to the King's house at Port/Royall, "from thence to the Church, & after a sermon was carried "to the Pallisadoes & there buried. All the forts fired "an equal number of guns, wee fired two & twenty & "after wee & the Drake had fired, all the merchant men "fired."

Jamaica was Morgan's chosen home and there he was buried and there his will was filed in the Record Office at Spanish Town. It makes intelligent and appropriate provision for his wife and near relatives.

Morgan was not an ordinary man. He was a brave and skilful leader, quick in thought and in action. He was impulsive, generous, perhaps not over/scrupulous, and as was natural was impatient of restraint. The charges of cruelty cannot be considered as fully proven by Exque/melin's statements, but it can be assumed that his wild crew committed many excesses. A pirate he certainly was not. Always a loyal servant to his King and country, his own ambitions never were at variance with what he considered to be for England's good. If he was on occasion a roisterer, he was certainly a generous and open-handed one; a man who compelled popularity and encouraged enmities. The effect of his greatness on the events of his time was superior to the harm done by his defects.

CHAPTER IV

ADMIRALS DE POINTIS AND DU CASSE

BRITISH seamen were not the only ones to disturb the tranquillity of the Spanish possessions. Neither the death of Morgan nor the ban placed upon buccaneering by the English King gave security to the ports of the Spanish Main. In order to understand the full significance of the attack upon Cartagena by the French in 1697, it is necessary to review the condition of Europe at the time.

In October, 1685, Louis XIV deprived the Huguenots of the privileges conferred upon them by the Edict of Nantes. Churches were destroyed, ministers exiled, and the reformed worship forbidden. Although these measures did not, as it later appeared, commend themselves to Pope Innocent XI, they received the approbation of a considerable portion of the Catholic world. The Protestant nations made no effort, however, to disguise their alienation from France, and, forgetting for the time their own minor differences, concluded in July, 1686, a defensive alliance at Augsburg. Grievances other than those based on religious prejudices were exploited and this league included Austria, Spain, Holland, Sweden, Saxony, Bavaria, and most of the German and Italian States. By this Alliance of Augsburg, and by the fall of the

Catholic government of James II in England in 1688, all
Europe was combined against Louis XIV.

War was declared by France on England, Holland,
Austria, and Spain. With marvellous energy Louis undertook the task of defending himself. He was attacked
on the south by Spain; on the northeast by the combined
forces of Holland, Germany, and the Spanish Nether-
lands; on the southeast by the Italians, and his coast
towns were constantly threatened by the English and
Dutch. Even the extraordinary resources of France could
not long sustain this unequal conflict, and in May, 1697,
negotiations looking toward peace were opened at Ryswick. The Peace Conferences were long, tedious, and difficult, the numerous contracting parties and their mutual
differences making a satisfactory conclusion of the con-
ference well-nigh impossible. Spain was not desirous to
end the war, and it was not until the news that Barcelona
had surrendered to the French under the Duke of Ven-
dôme, and that Cartagena, the stronghold of Spain in the
New World, had been taken by de Pointis, that Spain
made the necessary concessions which insured peace. On
the twentieth of September, 1697, the Treaty of Ryswick was signed by France, Spain, England, and Holland,
and on the thirtieth of October Austria made a separate
treaty of peace with France.

The expedition against Cartagena was the only effective offensive use to which French vessels were put dur-

ing this war, and that the blow against Spain was struck, and this so effectively, at such a distance from the actual field of expected hostilities, is an instructive example of the influence of sea-power.

This naval expedition was in itself interesting, and, in view of its size and effect, unique; inasmuch as it was actually a privateering undertaking. Early in the progress of the war a commodore in the French Navy, Baron de Pointis,* had suggested the sending out of a squadron under royal license, but privately equipped, for the pur-pose of striking a blow at Spanish power in America and at the same time gaining rich booty for those promoting and engaged in the enterprise. Finally, the exigencies of the war brought about the laying up of the Toulon fleet at Brest, and de Pointis, through Pontchartrain, then Minister of Marine, obtained the King's approbation of a plan by which the King was to lend to de Pointis ships, men, and ammunition, in return for a share of the ex-pected profits. The funds to cover the expenses of the expedition, it was agreed, should be provided by the pub-lic sale of shares. The public took kindly to the plan, and subscriptions poured in until interrupted by rumours of an expected peace, which caused anxiety as to the chances of profitable returns. In view of peace having been made with Savoy, de Pointis himself appears to have had some doubts as to whether a premature ending of the

---

* Jean Bernard Louis Desjean, Baron de Pointis, born 1645, died 1707.

war would not prevent the carrying out of his plans, and entered into an understanding with His Majesty that re/ imbursement would be made if peace should be con/ cluded before the sailing of the squadron. Even this, however, did not revive enthusiasm in the undertaking, and de Pointis had to content himself with a lesser num/ ber of ships than he had intended, in order to make the funds at his disposal meet the cost of the preparations.

In October, 1696, de Pointis began to fit out his fleet at Brest, and on the seventh of January, 1697, at day/ light, with his squadron he left that port, successfully eluding the English and Dutch blockading fleet. A short stop was made at Bertheaume to take on additional pro/ visions from certain vessels which had not arrived at Brest in season and which de Pointis had ordered to this ren/ dezvous; the squadron then proceeded toward Santo Domingo in the West Indies.

Santo Domingo, as the French settlements in His/ paniola were called, was the headquarters of the French buccaneers and filibusters, who at this period, with full official connivance, were preying upon the Spanish and English possessions and vessels. Part of the arrangement between de Pointis and the French Minister of Marine had been that the expedition should have the active sup/ port and co/operation of the Governor of Santo Domingo, and long before the squadron had sailed from Brest, in/ structions had been sent out to the Governor, M. du

Casse, to raise twelve hundred men to assist in the ex/
pedition. The regular force under M. du Casse was small,
and to furnish the number demanded meant necessarily
to enlist the services of the buccaneers. He finally assem/
bled and with difficulty held together until the somewhat
tardy arrival of de Pointis, a force made up of nearly seven
hundred buccaneers, one hundred and seventy soldiers
from the garrison, and enough colonists and negroes to
bring the total number up to about one thousand men.
For their proper conveyance he had provided seven ves/
sels of good size and a few smaller craft.

For convenience in this narrative the term "bucca/
"neers" will be often used to include this whole contin/
gent from Santo Domingo.

Owing to the co/operation given by M. du Casse in
this expedition, in which he figured as a leader of the
buccaneers, he has often been referred to in popular nar/
ratives as a buccaneer himself. Jean Baptiste du Casse was
an able French naval commander, born at Bern in 1640.
He was appointed Governor of Santo Domingo in 1691.
Shortly after his participation in the capture of Cartagena,
he returned to France and took part in the battle with the
English fleet commanded by Admiral Benbow in 1702.
During the War of Succession he commanded the French
naval forces at the attack on Barcelona in 1714.

Early in March, after a voyage of fifty/five days, de
Pointis arrived with his squadron at Cape Francis, Santo

Domingo, and there learned with some vexation that three French ships, to whose commanders he brought orders to attach themselves to his squadron, had sailed eight days before for France.

Although a brave and skilful officer, de Pointis appeared to lack the quality of sharing either the credit of successes or the responsibilities of command with others, and it appears to have been due to the disinterested loyalty of du Casse that the quarrels between the two commanders did not render the co-operation of the buccaneers impossible, and otherwise damage the expedition. The irritation incident to the continued lessening of his forces below the number fixed by de Pointis in his original plans was not an unlikely cause of much of the trouble, but whatever the cause, it is clear that he treated du Casse with less than the respect to which his position and abilities entitled him. M. du Casse, however, behaved with great moderation, and believing that by his own presence only could the troops which he had gotten together be kept within bounds, he volunteered to go with the expedition. This offer de Pointis accepted, but stipulated that du Casse should go with the simple rank of Captain, which he actually held in the French navy.

Before the squadron sailed, and in fact before the buccaneers would agree to join under de Pointis, it was necessary to arrive at a formal agreement as to the sharing of booty. It was mutually agreed "that the buccaneers and "colonists should, man for man, have the same shares of "booty that were allowed to the men on the King's "ships." This same arrangement was made with the ship's companies of several other vessels which joined the squadron.

After taking on provisions and aiding in equipping the vessels of the buccaneers, de Pointis ordered his ships to sail on the nineteenth of March, with directions to rendezvous off Cape Tiberon on the western extremity of Hispaniola. Owing to violent north winds this was made somewhat difficult, and it was not until the twenty-eighth of March that the squadron came together. At this place definite plans for the attack to be made upon Cartagena were adopted. Du Casse advised attacking Puerto Bello instead, because of his belief that certain richly laden ships were almost certainly there at the time, and because of the lesser strength of the fortresses at Puerto Bello. De Pointis, however, who had made up his mind in any event to ultimately attack Cartagena, and therefore feared to waste his provisions and incur other risks by a digression to Puerto Bello, persisted in his original plan, and the squadron sailed for Cartagena at once.

The vessels and men under de Pointis were as follows:

"Scepter," eighty-four guns, six hundred and fifty men, Captain Guillotin (flag-ship).

"St. Lewis," sixty-four guns, four hundred and twenty men, Vice-Admiral Levy.

"Fort," seventy guns, four hundred and fifty men, Rear-Admiral Viscount Coetlogon.

"Vermandois," sixty guns, three hundred and fifty men, commanded by Dubuison Gombaud.

"Apollo Furieux," sixty guns, three hundred and fifty men, commanded by La Motte Michel.

"St. Michael," sixty guns, three hundred and fifty men, commanded by le Chev. de Marolles.

"Christ," forty-four guns, two hundred and twenty men, commanded by le Chev. de la Motte d'Heran.

"Avenant," thirty guns, two hundred men, commanded by le Chev. Francine.

"Marin," twenty-eight guns, one hundred and eighty men, commanded by St. Vandrille.

"Eclatant," bomb vessel, sixty men, commanded by De Mons.

"Providence," four guns, thirty men, commanded by le Chev. de L'Escovet.

"Pontchartrain," forty guns, one hundred men.

—— (frigate), twenty-four guns, sixty men — together with six mortar boats and other craft.

On board of these vessels were one hundred and ten officers, fifty-five marines, twenty-one hundred seamen and seventeen hundred and fifty soldiers, or a total of four thousand and fifteen men.

In addition to these ships and men there were the seven vessels classed by de Pointis as frigates, of from eight to twenty-four guns each, and carrying the approximately one thousand men furnished by du Casse. The total com-bined forces of the expedition were about five thousand, and the number of vessels twenty, exclusive of six to ten very small craft.

Before sailing from Cape Tiberon, de Pointis issued the orders necessary for the division of command both at sea and on shore, and arranged the relative authority and seniority, a somewhat troublesome matter, which his va-rious vessel commanders were to have when in command as land officers. Du Casse was definitely given command of the buccaneers, who were made into one troop, the ships' crews being made up into companies, and divided into battalions.

Before leaving France, de Pointis had received from Paris plans and directions regarding the port and fortresses of Cartagena, and detailed instructions as to the best method of attack. In many ways the information given was after-wards proved inaccurate and at the time conflicted with that furnished by du Casse. The plans of de Pointis were, nevertheless, greatly helped by the information which he received in advance, and he appears to have been fully alive to the importance of first securing certain strategic points of great advantage to either those defending or at-tacking the place. In particular it had been pointed out to him that it would be necessary for him to obtain early the command of the only road to the interior from Cartagena, in order to prevent the removal of treasure from Cartagena during the progress of his attack upon the city itself. He had therefore resolved to land the troop of buc' caneers the very night of his arrival off Cartagena, with the purpose of having them secure possession of La Popa, the high hill behind the town, overlooking the town it' self and the road leading from it. With this plan in mind he anchored his fleet about twelve miles to the eastward on the thirteenth of April. The selection of the bucca' neers for this dangerous and arduous task created some feeling between them and de Pointis, who accused them, rather unjustly, of a lack of bravery. Du Casse agreed to lead them, and preparations were made for their landing; but the heavy surf, not unusual at that time of year, made even an attempt impracticable, and de Pointis himself was nearly drowned while searching for a proper landing' place. He reluctantly decided that the city could be ap' proached with safety from the harbour side only, and sailed the morning of the fourteenth toward the entrance to the harbour, called Boca Chica. His ships were fired upon from the city walls as they passed by, showing the pres' ence there of many heavy guns. This firing did slight damage to the rigging of a few of the vessels and killed three men; it was not returned by the guns of the ships, as de Pointis did not feel sufficiently assured as to the depth of the water to order any of his ships near enough inshore to effectively return the fire.

In the obscurity of the night of the fifteenth, recon-
noissance was made to select a landing on Tierra Bomba,
near the Boca Chica Fort, and on the sixteenth, under
cover of firing from the ships, which held the enemy's
attention elsewhere, about one thousand troops were
landed. During this operation a small boat, of a size to
carry about sixty men, was captured, and from one of the
prisoners taken de Pointis learned that the galleons for
the capture of which du Casse had urged him to go to
Puerto Bello, were still at that port. Among the prisoners
were two Franciscan friars, one of whom was despatched
to the commandant of Boca Chica Fort to demand its surrender, which was refused. During the day a re-enforce-
ment of three hundred men was sent from the city to the
fort, and an attack upon them by the buccaneers from
the shore brought on a brief general engagement, resulting in the surrender of the fort by its aged Commandant D. Sancho Jimeno, to whom was given the courteous
and generous treatment to which he was entitled by the
gallantry of his defence. The loss of the French and buccaneers in this engagement is reported by de Pointis to
have been fifty, and that of the Spanish as ninety. The
Spanish accounts, however, state that the whole garrison
amounted to seventy only.

The fort was immediately occupied and garrisoned by
the French troops, while six hundred and fifty of the
buccaneers were immediately (on the seventeenth) sent

across the outer harbour, or Bay of Cartagena, with orders to land and seize La Popa if possible. Du Casse was unable, on account of a wound received, to accompany the buccaneers, who went under command of Captain Daunou. La Popa was discovered by the buccaneers, after some resistance on the road, to have been abandoned by the Spanish.

While this expedition was in progress the ships entered the bay, and on the morning of the eighteenth began the bombardment of Fort Santa Cruz at one side of the entrance to the inner harbour. This passage had on the previous day been practically closed by the Spanish through the sinking of three or four vessels. During this bombardment the troops which had been landed at Boca Chica (and which now numbered about two thousand) had, under the personal leadership of de Pointis, been marching overland * toward the town. Upon their approach to Fort Santa Cruz, the garrison, fearing to be cut off, deserted the fort and fled into Cartagena. Finding an assault upon the defences of the town on the side toward the sea impracticable, de Pointis had the troops which had arrived from Boca Chica transported across the bay early on the nineteenth, and with these troops he joined the buccaneers near San Lázaro. After a thorough re-

* Boca Grande, at one time a broad entrance into the bay from the sea between the island of Tierra Bomba and the neck of land extending from the mainland to the westward, appears at this time to have been actually closed for its full breadth and to have offered a road for the passage of the troops.

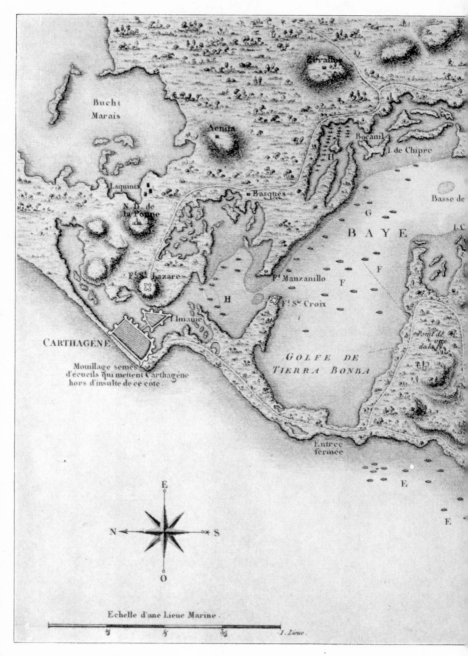

Bucht
Marais

Zevallos

Acuita

Bocanil
I. de Chipre

Laquinta

N. D. de
la Pomme

Basques

Basse de

G

B A Y E

I. C.

F

F

Ft St Lazare

H

Pt Manzanillo

F

Ft Ste Croix

Point de
la B.

L'Imane

CARTHAGÉNE

Mouillage semés
d'écueils qui mettent Carthagène
hors d'insulte de ce côté.

GOLFE DE
TIERRA BONBA

Entrée
fermée

E

E

E

E

N

S

O

Echelle d'une Lieue Marine.

1. Lieue.

DE POINTIS' MAP OF

PRISE
DE CARTHAGÊNE
DES INDES
PAR L'ESCADRE FRANÇAISE
AUX ORDRES DE POINTIS
en 1697.

LEGENDE
Pour les opérations du Siège

A. *Position de l'Escadre Française le 14 Avril.*
B. *Chaloupes des troupes de débarquements pour l'attaque du Fort Boucachique par terre.*
C. *Deux Vaisseaux canonnant le même Fort pour favoriser le débarquement des troupes.*
D. *Galiote à bombe tirant également sur ce Poste qui se rend après deux jours de résistance.*
E. *Batiments Flibustiers et autres, faisants partie de l'Armée française.*
F. *L'Armée mouillée devant le Fort St Croix que les Espagnols abandonnent.*
G. *Navire Flibustiers sur leurs ancres.*
H. *Lieu du Débarquement des Flibustiers pour l'attaque du Couvent de Notre Dame de la Poupe et du Fort St Lazare.*

ETAT DES VAISSEAUX
ET DE CAPITAINES
Qui composoient la Flote.

Le Sceptre	M. De Pointis.
Le St Louis	De Levy.
Le Vermandois	Du Buisson.
L'Apollon	De Gombaut.
Le Furieux	De la Mothe.
La Mutine	De Massiac.
L'Avenent	De Francine.
Le Marin	De Vaudrille.
Le Fort	Le Vte De Goitlogon.
Le St Michel	De Maroles.
Le Pontchartrain	De Mornai d'Amblevil.
La Française de St Malo	De la Ville-au-Glamas.

THE TAKING OF CARTAGENA IN 1697

connoissance both de Pointis and du Casse were convinced that this fort so effectually commanded the city that no at/ tempt could be made to capture it until the fort had been taken. It was decided to reach the fort from the direction of La Popa and to mine it, but the strength of the ex/ pected resistance appears to have been over/estimated, as shortly after the beginning of a spirited attack upon the fort, to which a feeble return fire was made, the garrison took advantage of the absence of troops upon the side op/ posite to the attackers, and abandoned the fort. De Pointis in his report of this engagement states that he found only nine killed and wounded within the fort, and that of his own troops one officer and five men were killed and two officers wounded.

Near the bottom of the walls of San Lázaro a narrow causeway and bridge, now called the Puenta Media Luna, connects the mainland with the outer town or suburb of Cartagena, called Getsemani, well protected on the side toward the land by strong walls. The French troops were advanced to this bridge, fascines built, artillery from the ships landed, and on the twenty/eighth active opera/ tions against the town began. Of the twenty/seven guns landed, several were of the heaviest then known, and six of the large ones were placed only a little more than one hundred yards from the gate. During these preparations, the ships, although somewhat undermanned, owing to the large numbers of men engaged on shore, had en/

deavoured to effectively bombard the town from the harbour, but had not been able to get near enough to do
any great damage, nor could their fire reach the bastion
against which the land forces were directing their efforts.
After some days of more or less continuous firing by the
guns of lesser size, de Pointis on the twenty-ninth, having
his larger guns now in position, appointed the thirtieth
for a grand combined assault by both the troops and ships.
Du Casse, however, on the twenty-ninth, from a position
he had taken at the end of one of the trenches, saw clearly
a breach in the walls, in strengthening which the Spaniards were hurriedly engaged. Upon his report and advice, de Pointis decided to press the attack at that point,
which was done, and with such good effect that on the
thirtieth of April both buccaneers and French pressed
through, driving the Spanish troops before them toward
the gates of the city. The Spanish troops, however, were
obliged to make one more stand against the attacking
forces, as the Governor of Cartagena refused to open the
gates to them until they had attacked the French troops
in Getsemani. Against their forced and somewhat unex-
pected assault the French troops fell back for a few mo-
ments, but rallying, drove them again toward the city
gates, which this time were opened to them. The loss to
the Spanish troops upon the walls and during the retreat
through the streets of Getsemani is reported to have been
very heavy, and without counting the earlier losses which

were more difficult to determine, de Pointis stated that he found over one hundred and fifty pierced with bayo/ nets in this last engagement. His own losses he reported to be sixty killed and rather more than that number wounded.

On the first of May preparations were made for at/ tacking the town itself, both from the land and from the ships. On the second, the bombardment began, and after three hours' firing the Governor asked for terms. At first de Pointis refused, but through a friendly Indian, and also by a messenger from one of his officers left at Boca Chica, who had been reconnoitring on the mainland, he learned of the approach from the interior of two re/enforcing troops of about one thousand men each; this news made de Pointis more ready to treat.

The news of the fall of Getsemani apparently reached the relieving forces, who, believing it too late to render effective help, kept clear of the city. On the third, Car/ tagena capitulated on the following terms, in the making of which du Casse appears to have tried to exercise a moderating influence:

That all public effects and office accounts should be delivered to the captors.

That merchants should produce their books of ac/ counts, and deliver up all money and effects held by them for their correspondents.

That every inhabitant should be free to leave the town,

or to remain in his dwelling. That those who retired should first deliver up all their property to the captors. That those who remained should declare faithfully, under penalty of entire confiscation, the gold, silver, and jewels in their possession; on which condition, and upon deliv﹣ering up one﹣half, they should be permitted to retain the other half and afterwards be regarded as subjects of France.

That the churches and religious houses should be spared and protected.

Some days were taken in preparations for the evacua﹣tion by the Spanish and it was not until the sixth day after the surrender that the Spanish commander, Count Ugnez de los Rois, with about twenty﹣eight hundred men, marched out through two files of the French soldiers and seamen and the buccaneers.

It has been alleged, particularly by Spanish historians, that the Governor of Cartagena acted traitorously in mak﹣ing this capitulation, and that he was bribed by de Pointis. There does not appear, however, to be any evidence to substantiate this.

The problem to secure possession of the large amount of silver in the town and at the same time to prevent unwarranted pillaging by the troops, especially by the buccaneers, was a serious one. De Pointis recognizing the control which du Casse had proved himself to have over the buccaneers, and appreciating too the upright﹣ness of his character, appointed du Casse Governor of

Cartagena. Notwithstanding all precautions, however, a considerable amount of private looting both by officers and men took place.

For the orderly, and, so far as possible, certain way of securing the treasure held in the city, de Pointis publicly declared that one tenth part of whatever was honestly brought to him would be returned to the proprietors, and also a tenth part given to the informers of all that should be secured by information given of those who had not declared their effects. This expedient appears to have been particularly successful, although the total amount received was less than had been expected. The news of the expedition had been heralded along the coast sufficiently in advance for much of the valuable property to have been removed before the approach of the French fleet.

The amount of gold and silver stated by de Pointis to have been collected amounted to between eight and nine millions, whether crowns or livres, de Pointis does not say. Du Casse believed the amount secured to be above twenty million livres.

It is not to be supposed that this sum was collected without friction nor without the exercise of that rigid authority which the possession of absolute power gave de Pointis; on the whole, however, reasonable moderation appears to have been used, and the stipulations of the capitulation treaty adhered to with as much care as the circumstances made possible.

The climate, to which the troops were unused, supple/mented by their excesses, brought on an epidemic of a contagious distemper, so that in six days' time eight hun/dred men were affected, a large proportion of whom died. The losses occasioned by this distemper and from other causes made the question of manning the ships for depar/ture a difficult one, and raised new differences between de Pointis and du Casse, which were augmented by dis/putes over the sharing of the booty.

Under the provisions of the agreement made before leaving Cape Tiberon, du Casse claimed for the bucca/neers and himself a one/quarter part of the eight millions. To learn from de Pointis that under the arrangement with the King, a tenth part only of the first million and a thir/tieth part of the sum remaining, was all that could be allotted to the whole body of men, was a great disappoint/ment to him, and at once brought about almost open hos/tilities. Instead of the two millions they had expected, the share allotted to the buccaneers was actually forty thousand crowns. The rage of du Casse was intense, and but for the fact that de Pointis had already put the treasure aboard his ships and arranged to man them without help from the buccaneers, serious trouble might not have been averted. In doing this, de Pointis was forced, on account of his great losses in men, to sail with a lesser fleet, aban/doning some of the undesirable ships, and leaving others for the use of the buccaneers.

Distressed as he was by this unsatisfactory settlement, and by the feeling that he had been treated unfairly, du Casse appears to have done his best to prevent disturb-ances, and kept back the statement of the accounting from his men until they were themselves all embarked. On the thirtieth of May, on the eve of sailing, de Pointis was stricken with the distemper, and giving over the command to Vice-Admiral Levy, ordered him to steer for Cape Tiberon. Meanwhile, the ships had completed the ruin of the fort at Boca Chica, and on the thirty-first the squad-ron put to sea.

Upon the departure of the French ships and the full realization of the small allotment of plunder they had re-ceived, the buccaneers first wished to follow and capture the flag-ship of de Pointis, and might indeed have tried and possibly accomplished their purpose had not one among them suggested that they immediately return and again plunder Cartagena. This resolution was made with-out consulting du Casse, who had sailed on the "Pont-"chartrain," with the determination of going first to Santo Domingo and then to France to demand redress from the King. When he learned the purpose of the buccaneers, he sent back orders for them to desist; but the possibility of immediate success overbalanced the weight of his influ-ence. On the first of June both de Pointis and du Casse had sailed, and the buccaneers returned and took posses-sion of Cartagena without the possibility of resistance, demanding five million livres as the price of their renewed departure. In four days this sum was nearly raised, showing that the more orderly methods of de Pointis had not wholly stripped the town of its wealth.

After a stop of about three days the buccaneers again sailed, making up a squadron of nine vessels. When less than one hundred miles on their course toward Santo Domingo, they were sighted by an English and Dutch fleet which had been sent out to intercept de Pointis. The French squadron had, however, been able to escape them on account of superior sailing, but the buccaneers were less fortunate, two of their richest ships were taken and two others driven on shore. On its way to France the squadron under de Pointis, who early recovered his health, barely escaped capture several times, but finally arrived at Brest, on the twenty-ninth of August, 1697.

The news of the victory at Cartagena, as has been already noted, materially helped to end the war, and within three weeks after the arrival home of the fleet, peace was declared.

The seal of official sanction was not only stamped upon this expedition at its inception, but the royal approval of the employment of the filibusters and buccaneers was given at its close. Du Casse was decorated and thanked by the French King.

A suit was brought in France on behalf of the buccaneers and the others who had engaged in the expedition under du Casse, and they were finally awarded the sum of four hundred thousand livres.* It is said, however, that the bulk of this was consumed in expenses and lost through the dishonesty of those who handled it.

* The Minister of Marine by direction of the King wrote to du Casse : "qu'il lui permettait de porter la croix de Saint Louis, quoiqu'il ne fût pas reçu ; "que Sa Majesté avait fait rendre justice aux habitants et filibustiers, que par la "convention faite entre le chevalier de Galliffet et les interessés de l'armement, "il leur reviendrait quatre cent mille livres, suivant l'arrêt du Conseil d'Etat, "dont copie lui était envoyée, que partie de cette somme serait délivrée en ar-"gent, partie en marchandises, munitions et nègres."

CHAPTER V

ADMIRAL VERNON

THE somewhat uncertain peace brought about in Europe in 1736, largely through the efforts of Sir
Robert Walpole, served to strengthen the family compact
between the Bourbon Courts of France and Spain and to
give time for the increase of the naval forces of these
countries, rather than to encourage, as Walpole had hoped,
a continued tranquillity.

The great sea-power of England had made possible
the development of a large English trade with Spanish
America during the alliance of England and Spain in the
war against France. This growing commercial supremacy
of England was naturally unwelcome to Spain, and both
by enforcing the limitations placed upon trading, inserted
in the Treaty of Utrecht, and by annoying restrictions in
the Spanish ports of America, Philip endeavoured to re-
duce to almost a disappearing point English intercourse
with the Spanish colonies.

English trading vessels, always at that time partially
armed, had frequent encounters with Spanish vessels, and
on neither side were the agreed-upon stipulations duly
respected. Walpole, more prudent than the adventurous
traders of England believed consistent with the honour
of his country, vainly tried to hold down the clamourers

for war in Parliament. The final event which made the efforts of Walpole wholly powerless for peace had its basis in the seizure off the Spanish Main, by the ship "Isabel," of an English merchant ship loaded with contraband stuffs, under Captain Jenkins. The commander of the "Isabel" appears to have treated Captain Jenkins with unusual cruelty, and before releasing him cut off one of his ears. In the spring of 1739, actually some years after the event, there was displayed, amid great excitement, to the members of the House of Commons, what may have been the mangled ear of Robert Jenkins. The pressure was too great, Walpole had to give way, and on the fif' teenth of June, 1739, war was declared against Spain.*

* DECLARATION OF WAR IN 1739

Trusty and well Beloved — We greet you Well —

Whereas several unjust seizures have been made and depredations carried on in the West Indies by Spanish Guarda Costas and Ships acting under the Commission of the King of Spain or his Governors contrary to the Treatys subsisting between us and the Crown of Spain and to the Law of Nations to the Great prejudice of the lawfull Trade & Commerce of our subjects; and many crueltys and barbaritys have been exercised on the Persons of such our subjects whose vessels have been so seized by the said Spanish Guarda Costas; And whereas frequent complaint has been made to the Court of Spain of these unjust practices and no satisfaction or Redress been procured; and whereas a Convention for makeing reparation to our subjects for the losses sustained by them on account of the unjust seizure & Captures above-mentioned was concluded between Us and the King of Spain on the 14th day of January last, N.S., by which convention it was stipulated that a certain sum of money should be paid at London within a Term specified in the sd. Convention as a balance due on the part of Spain to the Crown and subjects of Great Britain which Term did expire on the 25th day of May last and the paymt of the said sum agreed by the sd Convention has not been made according to the Stipulation for that purpose, by

Among the members of Parliament concerned in this demonstration and violently opposed to the Ministry, as well as equally violently urging a war of reprisal against Spain, was Captain Edward Vernon, a naval officer, who urged that an immediate expedition be sent out against Puerto Bello; he vigorously asserted that it could not only be captured, but pledged himself to take it with six ships

which means the Convention above-mentioned has been manifestly violated & Broke by the King of Spain and our Subjects remain without any Satisfaction or reparation for the many Great & Grievous losses sustained by them : We have tho't fit for ye vindicating the Honour of Our Crown & for procuring Reparation and Satisfaction for our Injured subjects to order Reprisals to be made upon the Crown & subjects of Spain. And We do therefore by virtue of these presents authorize & impower you to issue forth and grant Commissions of Marque & Reprisals to any of our loveing subjects or others who shall apply to you for the same and whom you shall deem fitly qualified in that behalf, For Armeing and fiting out Private Ships of War for the apprehending, seizing and taking the Ships, vessels & goods belonging to the King of Spain, his vassals & subjects or any inhabiting within his Countrys Territories & Dominions in the West Indies.

Provided always that before any such Commission or Commissions be Issued forth, security be given upon such Commission as hath been used in such cases. And you shall insert in every Commission to be so granted by you all such clauses and give such Directions & Instructions to the Person or Persons to whom you shall grant such Commissions as have been usual in cases of the like nature. And for so doing this shall be your warrant. And so we bid you farewell.

Given at our Court at Kensington the fifteenth day of June 1739, in the thirteenth year of our Reign.

By his Majesty's Command

HOLLIS NEWCASTLE

Superscribed "To our Trusty & Well Beloved Jonathan [Belcher] Esq., "our Capt. General & Govt in chief of our Provinces of the Massa. Bay and "NewHampshire in America & in his Absence to our Commander in Chief "or to the President of Council of our said Province for the time being."

only. In order more clearly to appreciate the bearing of
the influence of Vernon upon the events of this time, and
more particularly upon the expedition associated with his
name, it is necessary to glance at the record of his previ⁄
ous career. He appears to have had an amount of influ⁄
ence in the House of Commons, and a popular favour
outside, which made it impossible for the minister to
whom he was opposed to ignore either the plans he pro⁄
posed or his own offer to command the expedition.

Edward Vernon was the second son of James Vernon,
Secretary of State to William III, and was born in West⁄
minster the twelfth of November, 1684. After a thorough
study of the classics and the mathematical sciences, he was
allowed by his family to yield to a natural taste for the
sea, and entered the navy in 1701. He was with Admiral
Hopson in the "Torbay" at Vigo, the twelfth of October,
1702, and was second lieutenant on the "Resolution" in
the expedition against Hispaniola commanded by Captain
Walker. Afterwards he served with distinction with Ad⁄
miral Sir George Rook and with Sir Cloudesley Shovel.
His first command as captain was of the "Jersey," in
which he was sent to Port Royal, Jamaica, and for three
years had a successful career on the West Indian station,
capturing many prizes. This was followed by many years
of more important commands, chiefly in the Baltic, inter⁄
spersed with intervals of serving in the House of Com⁄
mons. It was the belief in England that if Puerto Bello

and Cartagena were taken, the Spanish power in the New World would be irredeemably broken, and shortly after the declaration of war Vernon was given a commission as Vice-Admiral of the Blue, and placed in command of a squadron of ships of war to be sent to the West Indies. His instructions were "To destroy the Spanish settle-"ments in the West Indies and to distress their shipping "by any method whatever."

The squadron consisted of the "Burford" of seventy guns and five hundred men, "Lenox" of seventy guns and four hundred and eighty men, "Elizabeth" of sev-enty guns and four hundred and eighty men, "Kent" of seventy guns and four hundred and eighty men, "Worces-"ter" of sixty guns and four hundred men, "Strafford" of sixty guns and four hundred men, "Princess Louisa" of sixty guns and four hundred and twenty men, "Nor-"wich" of fifty guns and three hundred men, and "Pearl" of forty guns and two hundred and forty men, in all nine ships carrying a total of five hundred and fifty guns and thirty-seven hundred men.

Admiral Vernon sailed from Portsmouth the twenty-third of July, 1739, and after some delays and digressions, occasioned chiefly by an unsuccessful search for a squad-ron of the enemy near the Spanish coast, arrived at Port Royal, Jamaica, the twelfth of October. With this as a base the Admiral proposed to attack Puerto Bello and Car-tagena, with such of his squadron as he had remaining,

ADMIRAL VERNON

several vessels having been detached for special service to harass the Spanish merchantmen. The ships remaining were the "Burford," "Princess Louisa," "Worcester," "Strafford," and "Norwich," and to these the Admiral was able to add at Port Royal the "Hampton Court" of seventy guns and four hundred and ninety/five men, and "Sheerness" of twenty guns and three hundred men, to/ gether with two hundred marines obtained from Gov/ ernor Trelawney.

On the fifth of November this squadron set sail, the "Sheerness" being sent as a scout in the direction of Car/ tagena, while the rest headed for Puerto Bello, off which port they lay to on the twentieth of that month. On the twenty/first he attacked the Iron Fort, so called, at the harbour's entrance, with his full strength at close range, and with such vigour that after a short but spirited re/ sistance it surrendered. The next morning while instruc/ tions were being given to govern the attack upon the re/ maining fortresses of San Jerónimo and Gloria Castle, a boat with a flag of truce came to the Admiral's ship, the result of which was a speedy capitulation on the follow/ ing terms dictated by Admiral Vernon:

"Articles of Capitulation granted by Edward Vernon, "Esq., Vice/Admiral of the Blue and Commander/in/ "Chief of His Majesty's Ships and Vessels in the West "Indies, and Commodore Brown; to Don Francisio Mar/ "tinez de Retey, Governor of Porto Bello, and Don Fran/

"cisio de Albaroa, Commandant of the Guarda Costas at
"the same place, the 22nd November, 1739, O.S.

" 1st Article. That the garrison be allowed to march
"out, as desired, upon condition the King of Great Brit/
"ain's troops be put into possession of Gloria Castle, be/
"fore four of the clock this evening, and the garrison to
"march out by ten of the clock to/morrow morning.

"That the inhabitants may either remove or remain,
"under the promise of security for themselves and their
"effects.

"2nd. That the Spanish soldiers may have a guard, if
"they think it necessary.

"3rd. They may carry off two cannons mounted with
"ten charges of powder for each, and their match lighted.

"4th. The gates of the Gloria Castle must absolutely
"be in possession of the King our master's troops by four
"of the clock, and the Spanish garrison shall remain in all
"safety for their persons or effects till the appointed time
"of their marching out, and to carry with them provi/
"sions and ammunition necessary for their safety.

"5th. That the ships with their apparel and arms, be
"absolutely delivered up to the use of his Brittanic Maj/
"esty; but that all the officers, both soldiers and crew,
"shall have three days allowed them to retire with all
"their personal effects; only one officer being admitted on
"board such ship and vessel, to take possession for the King
"our master, and see this article strictly complied with.

" 6th. That provided the Articles above mentioned are
" strictly complied with, and that possession be given of
"Castle St. Jeronimo in the same manner as is stipulated
"for the Castle Gloria, then the Clergy, the Churches
"and Town shall be protected and preserved in all their
"immunities and properties, and that all prisoners already
"taken shall be set at liberty before our leaving the port.

"Given under our hands on board his Majesty's ship
" BURFORD in Porto Bello harbour, the 22nd day of No-
"vember, 1739, O.S.

"E. Vernon

"Chas. Brown "

As a result of this capitulation, the English fleet secured two Spanish men-of-war of twenty guns each, one
other vessel, forty brass cannons, four brass mortars, eighteen smaller brass guns, a quantity of ammunition, and
about ten thousand dollars. The fortifications and some
eighty iron cannons were rendered useless before the departure of the squadron, which shortly returned to Jamaica.

As had been predicted, Puerto Bello was taken with *six*
ships, and when the news, which had been despatched
to London, reached there, the thanks of both Houses of
Parliament were voted to the Admiral.

The English reports of this victory state the number
of men taken to have been five officers and thirty-five

men "out of three hundred, the rest being either killed "or wounded or having made their escape "; the Spanish accounts, however, declare that Puerto Bello was defended by a total of thirty men and five cannons, and Spanish historians point with amusement to the celebration of this victory in London. The actual record of the number of cannons taken away, however, and other circumstances, make it appear improbable that the Spanish version is strictly correct, although it is equally probable that the English account exaggerates the strength of the Spanish garrison.

Whatever may have been the exact facts, the nation was intoxicated with joy at the news of the victory. That the forts were only partially manned was not known; the simple fact that Vernon's boast had been made good and Puerto Bello taken with six ships was the glorious news and all that was needed to make of him a popular hero. Hundreds of different medals were struck to commemorate the event.* Vernon was the idol of the hour.

On the twentyfifth of February, 1740, Admiral Vernon, after refitting his ships, sailed again from Jamaica for the Spanish Main, and from the sixth to the ninth of March bombarded Cartagena, doing some damage, but also receiving enough injuries to his smaller craft to make it expedient to sail to Puerto Bello to effect repairs. On the

* *Admiral Vernon Medals*, 1739–1742, by Dr. Malcolm Storer, Proc. Mass. Hist. Soc. April, 1919.

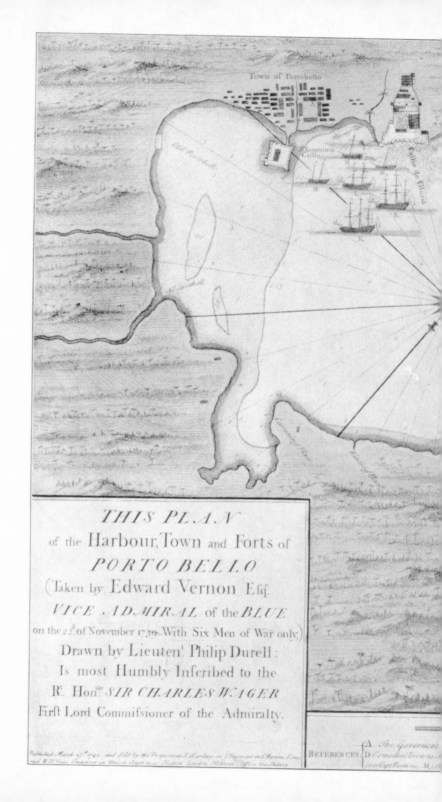

THIS PLAN
of the Harbour, Town and Forts of
PORTO BELLO
(Taken by Edward Vernon Esq.
VICE ADMIRAL of the *BLUE*
on the 22.d of November 1739. With Six Men of War only.)
Drawn by Lieuten.t Philip Durell:
Is most Humbly Inscribed to the
R.t Hon.ble *SIR CHARLES WAGER*
First Lord Commissioner of the Admiralty.

S.ᵗ Bona Aventura

Iron Castle

A Scale of Two English Miles

Salmadine

twenty-second of March he attacked Chagres, lying off
that place and keeping up a moderate but continual bombardment, until on the twenty-fourth the garrison capitulated. The ships engaged in the bombardment were the
"Strafford," "Norwich," "Falmouth," and "Princess
"Louisa." After seizing a considerable quantity of goods
of value from the custom-house stores, and taking on
board all serviceable brass cannons and other guns, the
custom-house was destroyed by fire, and on the thirtieth
the squadron sailed again for Jamaica.

That the strength of the Cartagena fortifications was
fully realized is clear from the fact that before he again
assaulted that place, Admiral Vernon remained almost
constantly for months at Jamaica, re-enforcing his squadron
with ships and men. Late in the year his squadron was
joined by a number of store ships under convoy, and by
transports with troops. In January, 1741, he was further
re-enforced by a squadron under Rear-Admiral Sir Chaloner Ogle, consisting, with those already arrived, of thirty
ships of the line and some ninety other vessels, the ships
manned by fifteen thousand sailors. The land troops sent
out from England amounted to about twelve thousand,
these latter being augmented at Jamaica by about thirty-
six hundred troops from the American colonies.*

* These American troops were made up as follows: from Massachusetts, five
companies ; Rhode Island, two companies ; Connecticut, two companies ;
New York, five companies ; New Jersey, three companies ; Pennsylvania,
eight companies ; Maryland, three companies ; Virginia, four companies ;

The command of the land troops had been given to Major-General Lord Cathcart, who unfortunately died before reaching Jamaica, and the command fell upon Brigadier-General Thomas Wentworth, who appears to have been particularly unsuited for the great responsibility thrust upon him.

The causes which led to the later practical failure of this expedition against Cartagena cannot be attributed to the lack of proper preparations or equipments, nor to the haste employed; indeed, the expedition appears to have been planned with the most careful regard to all details. Vessels were engaged in scout service to determine as clearly as possible the whereabouts of the French squadron under Admiral the Marquis d'Antin, and careful observations had been made of the fortifications about Cartagena, the prevalent weather conditions, currents, etc., as well as the depths of water off the town and at the Boca Chica forts. The instructions given to the fleet on sailing from Jamaica divided the fighting vessels into three divisions, one under Vice-Admiral Vernon (Commander-in-Chief), one under Rear-Admiral Sir Chaloner Ogle, and one under Commodore Lestock. The fleet comprised some thirty line-of-battle ships, twenty-two frigates, and a large miscellaneous squadron of transports, fire-ships,

North Carolina, four companies. Among other American officers was Colonel Laurence Washington, and it was on account of his association with Admiral Vernon that Mount Vernon subsequently received its name.

bomb-ketches * and tenders, in all one hundred and twenty-four sail.† Not unnaturally the rumours of these

* Small light draught vessels carrying one or more guns or mortars.

† SAILING AND FIGHTING INSTRUCTIONS GIVEN TO THE FLEET ON THEIR SAILING FROM JAMAICA, BY EDWARD VERNON, ESQ., VICE-ADMIRAL OF THE BLUE, AND COMMANDER-IN-CHIEF OF ALL HIS MAJESTY'S SHIPS AND VESSELS IN THE WEST INDIES

Line of Battle

The PRINCESS AMELIA to lead with the Starboard, and the SUFFOLK with the Larboard Tacks on Board. But if I shall find it necessary from the different Motions of the Enemy, to change our Order of Battle, to have those who are now appointed to lead on the Starboard Tack, to continue to lead the fleet on the Larboard Tack on our going about, or those now to lead on the Larboard Tack, on the contrary to do the same, as the Exigency of the Service may require ; I will, with my Signal for Tacking, hoist a Dutch Jack on the Flag Staff, under the Union Flag, the usual Signal for Tacking when they are to continue to lead the Fleets on their respective Tacks, accordingly.

Rear Admiral of the Blue, Sir Chaloner Ogle

Frigates	Rates	Ships Names	Captains	Men	Guns
	3d.	Princess Amelia	Hemmington	600	80
	4th.	Windsor	Berkley	400	60
Experiment		York	Coates	400	60
Sheerness	3d.	Norfolk	Graves	600	80
Vesuvius Fireship			Sir C. Ogle }	615	80
		Russel			
Terrible Bomb			Capt. Norris }		
Phaeton		Shrewsbury	Townsend	600	80
Goodley	4th.	Rippon	Jolley	400	60
		Litchfield	Cleveland	300	50
		Jersey	Lawrence	400	60
		Tilbury	Long	400	60

Vice-Admiral of the Blue, Vernon

Frigates	Rates	Ships Names	Captains	Men	Guns
Squirrel	3d.	Orford	Lt. Aug. Fitzroy	480	70
Shoreham	4th.	Princess Louisa	Stapleton	400	60
Eleanor		Augusta	Dennison	400	60
Seahorse		Worcester	Perry Mayne	400	60
Strumbolo	3d.	Chichester	Robert Trevor	600	80
Success		Princess Caroline	Adm. Vernon } Capt. Watson }	620	80
Vulcan		Torbay	Gascoigne	600	80
Cumberland	4th	Strafford	Tho. Trevor	400	60
Alderrey Bomb		Weymouth	Knowles	400	60
Pompey		Deptford	Moyston	400	60
Brig. Tender	3d.	Burford	Griffen	480	70

preparations for the attack on Cartagena, reached that
place weeks before the news became a certainty, through

Commodore Lestock's Division

Frigates	Rates	Ships Names	Captains	Men	Guns
	4th.	Defiance	John Trevor	400	60
		Dunkirk	Cooper	400	60
Astrea		Lyon	Cotterel	400	60
Wolf Sloop	3d.	Prince Frederic	Ld. A. Beauclerc	480	70
Aetna		Boyne	Com. Lestock ⎱ Capt. Colby ⎰	600	80
Firebrand		Hampton Court	Dent	480	70
Virgin Queen	4th.	Falmouth	Douglass	300	50
		Montague	Chambers	300	60
	3d.	Suffolk	Davers	480	70

Signals

When the Admiral would speak with the Captain of any Ship under-men-
tioned, he will raise a pendant, as against the Ship's name, and of the Colour
set above it; if a Lieutenant, the same Signal with a Weft of the Ensign;
and if a Boat without an Officer, the Weft will be hoisted but half Staff up.
Memorandum, when I would have any of the Fireships, Bombs or Tenders,
taken in tow at the same Time I make the Signal for the Ship that is to tow,
and for the Ship that is to be tow'd, I will hoist up a Flag Blue and White,
at the Flag-staff of the Main-top-mast-head.

Red	White	Blue	Yellow		
Boyne	Pss. Amelia	Chichester	Terrible	Main ⎫	
Norfolk	Suffolk	Shrewsbury	Elenor	Fore ⎬ top-Mast	
Worcester	Lyon	Defiance	Etna	Mizen ⎭ head	
Tilbury	Squirrel	Torbay	Firebrand	Starbd ⎱ Main-topsail	
Windsor	Pss. Louisa	Falmouth	Vesuvius	Larbd ⎰ Yard-Arm	
Burford	P. Frederick	Strafford	Phaeton	Starbd ⎱ Fore-topsail	
Montague	Orford	Weymouth	Strombolo	Larbd ⎰ Yard-arm	
Shoreham	Augusta	Pss. Caroline	Success	Starbd ⎱ Mizen-topsail	
Hamptoncourt	Dunkirk	Jersey	Vulcan	Larbd ⎰ Yard-arm	
Litchfield	Lud. Castle	Deptford	Cumberland	Starbd ⎱ Main-yard-	
Experiment	Rippon	York	Alderney	Larbd ⎰ arm	
Sea Horse	Sheerness	Russell	BrigTender	Starbd ⎱ Fore-yard-	
Astrea	Wolf		Virgin Qu.	Larbd ⎰ arm	
			Pompey	Starbd ⎱ Cross-jack-	
			Goodley	Larbd ⎰ yard-arm	

When the Ships are in Line of Battle, the Frigates, Fireships, Bombs and
Tenders, are to keep on the opposite Side of the Enemy, when I make the
Signal in Line of Battle, for the Van of the Fleet to tack first in order to gain
the Windward of the Enemy, then each Ship is to tack in the Head-most Ship's
weak, for losing no Ground. For all other Signals they are referr'd to the

the definite reports of a French ship which appears to have been sent to Cartagena by the French Admiral expressly to warn the inhabitants of the impending attack.

During the last week in January, 1741, the three divisions sailed from Port Royal, a few days apart, effecting a junction at sea on the thirty-first, and making Cape Tiberon, on the western extremity of Hispaniola (now the island of Haiti and San Domingo) on the seventh of February. After several days of careful reconnoitring to make certain whether or not the French fleet had sailed for Europe as reported, the three divisions came to anchor in the bays near the cape. On the twenty-fifth of February the fleet left for Cartagena under easy sail, and came to anchor on the fourth of March a few leagues to windward (that is, to the eastward) of the town of Cartagena, between that place and Punta Canoas. During several days detailed preparations for the attack were made, and various councils of war held, one of which settled the important matters relative to the distribution of the expected booty, and one confirming the Admiral's plan of attack. Great care seems to have been taken to obtain as complete plans as possible of the forts at Boca Chica, and careful soundings were made by some of the smaller vessels all along the Tierra Bomba shore and at the entrance to the harbour. A feint at landing on the

General printed Sailing and Fighting Instructions, and such other additional instructions as you received from me.

shore side of the town was made by some of the smaller vessels, apparently for the purpose, a hope to some extent realized, of engaging the attention of the enemy from the real landing-point at Boca Chica.

On the morning of the ninth, Sir Chaloner Ogle, with his division, moved forward to the attack, followed by Admiral Vernon with his division and all the transports, leaving the division under Commander Lestock at anchor. As the ships moving to leeward approached Boca Chica, the small fort of Chamba (on Tierra Bomba, east of Boca Chica Castle) fired a few shots, but was soon silenced and deserted. Three of the eighty-gun ships were anchored close to the forts of San Jago and San Felipe, and main-tained a very hot fire, so that these forts were soon de-serted; the evening of that day grenadiers were landed and took possession of them without meeting any resist-ance. Also during the evening, from the bomb-ketches and from those of the ships which could comfortably approach, a continual fire was kept up against Boca Chica Castle, which was returned with some spirit, under cover of which firing troops and artillery were landed during the night and next forenoon. The troops were encamped under the protection of a woody growth near, but appar-ently somewhat protected from, Boca Chica Castle. It was during and immediately after the landing of these troops that the serious differences of opinion between General Wentworth and Admiral Vernon began to arise,

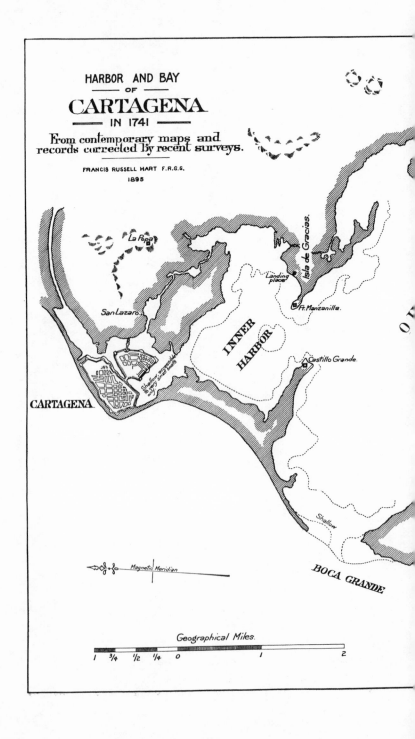

HARBOR AND BAY
— OF —
CARTAGENA
— IN 1741 —

From contemporary maps and
records corrected by recent surveys.

FRANCIS RUSSELL HART F.R.G.S.
1895

La Popa

Isla de Gracias.

Landing
place

San Lazaro.

Ft. Manzanilla.

INNER HARBOR

Castillo Grande.

CARTAGENA

Shallow accessible to very small boats

Magnetic Meridian

Shallow

BOCA GRANDE

Geographical Miles.

1   3/4   1/2   1/4   0   1   2

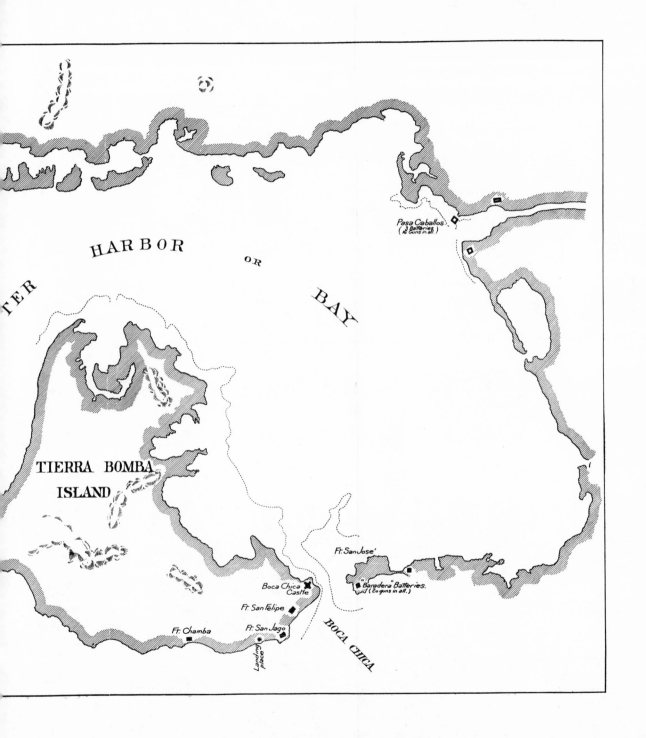

HARBOR OR BAY

TER

Pasa Caballos
(3 Batteries
18 Guns in all.)

TIERRA BOMBA
ISLAND

Ft: San Jose'

"Baradera" Batteries.
(20 guns in all.)

Boca Chica
Castle

Ft: San Felipe

Ft: Chamba   Ft: San Jago

Landing place

BOCA CHICA

differences which afterwards were to prove to a large extent the cause of the failure of the expedition, and which
served at once to create a most unfortunate feeling of an-
tagonism between the sea and land forces. The Admiral
complained of the delays of the troops to press the attack
upon the castle, and on the eleventh he and Sir Chaloner
Ogle joined in a letter to General Wentworth urging immediate action. That delays somewhat difficult to understand
did take place is evident from the fact that on the nineteenth, owing to complaints from General Wentworth,
several vessels undertook successfully, but with some difficulty, to silence the Baradera Battery on the opposite
side of the harbour entrance, the fire from which reached
the encampment of the troops, and on the twenty-first
of March, at a council of war of the naval commanders,
complaint as to the slow progress of the troops was for-
mally made. Finally, on the days from the twenty-fourth
to the twenty-sixth, by the co-operation of the vessels
and troops, both Boca Chica Castle and the San José fortress were taken, as was also one of the Spanish ships.
The San José fortress appears to have been almost deserted
when taken, and it is probable that this fort was not ac-
tively defended. That the defence of Boca Chica Castle
itself was gallant and spirited is certain from the clear record of the extensive operations against it. Before it was
taken, however, the defenders had largely made their
escape, and had found time to partially block the channel

up the bay by sinking the Spanish ships "Africa" and "San Carlos," and to burn the ship "San Felipe" on the shore.

During the next few days the fleet was able to enter the bay; the batteries at the small Passo Caballos entrance were easily destroyed and a safe anchorage established. The forts at Boca Chica were adequately garrisoned, the troops re-embarked, and preparations were made for the real attack upon the city.

The Spanish Viceroy, Lieutenant-General Don Sebastian de Eslaba, was resident at Cartagena, and the Governor of the city was Don Blas de Leso. According to contemporary Spanish accounts, the forces at the disposal of the Viceroy and Governor were eleven hundred veteran soldiers, three hundred militia, six hundred Indians, and two companies of negroes and free mulattoes. The naval forces in the harbour were six ships with six hundred seamen and four hundred soldiers, making about four thousand men in all. These are probably accurate estimates of the actual Spanish forces, and it is certain that the strength of the defence of the place was due to its well-built fortifications rather than to the number of its defenders, whose numbers were undoubtedly much fewer than the attacking forces. The Viceroy had ample notice of the coming of the attacking expedition, and concentrated his small forces at important points on the walls of the city itself and at San Lázaro, a strong fortress, built on a slight elevation, outside the walls, and guarding the approach to the city from the land side. The strategic importance of this fortress, and a general idea of the walls and other fortifications of Cartagena, can best be obtained by a glance at the maps.

It was considered essential by the attacking forces to first occupy San Lázaro, and indeed if this had been accom⁄plished it is probable that the remaining Spanish troops would have been insufficient to make any long effective resistance to an entrance into the city. At a council of war held on board the "Princess Caroline," on the thir⁄tieth of March, in Cartagena Harbour, in which the divi⁄sion commanders of both the sea and land forces took part, it was resolved to land the troops at a convenient point on the south side of the harbour, under protection of the guns of the ships; the first duty of the troops to be to cut off all land communications from the city. On the first few days of April troops were landed at Isla de Gracias close to Mansanilla Castle, from which a fairly good road reached into the town, passing under the walls of San Lázaro. This landing was made without opposition, the guns from the ships sweeping the country between Isla de Gracias and San Lázaro, and the landing⁄place being beyond the range of the guns at Castillo Grande; the rel⁄ative positions of these places and others referred to in this account are clearly indicated on the maps.

With the landing of the troops the dissensions between

the commanders of the land and sea forces began anew;
Admirals Vernon and Ogle appear to have constantly con-
demned the procrastination of General Wentworth and
urged the necessity for immediate action if serious ravages
of sickness among the troops were to be avoided; General Wentworth as constantly urged the necessity for more
efficient co-operation on the part of the fleet, asserting
that the ships should be brought into the inner harbour,
where the town itself and (more particularly) San Lázaro
would be within effective range of fire. The experiment
of sending one of the captured ships into the inner harbour was tried by Admiral Vernon, but the ship, although
apparently finding sufficient water, was finally of necessity abandoned, as unsupported it could not stand the close
fire from the city walls. This incident, which furnished
one of the prime causes of dispute among the respective
partisans of Admiral Vernon and General Wentworth,
both then and later in England, is easily understood by
those familiar with the harbour of Cartagena. The water
in the inner harbour is now, and undoubtedly was then,
too shallow to hold ships of the size of Vernon's fighting
vessels, but through a very narrow and twisting channel
it is quite possible that one or two ships might with careful piloting enter the inner harbour.

The friends of General Wentworth, in charging Admiral Vernon with neglect in this instance, were clearly
in the wrong, as were those also who supported General

Wentworth's claim that the fleet did not give its full sup/
port to his requests by preventing communication with
the town from the shore to the eastward. Admiral Ver/
non, when requested to do so by General Wentworth, ap/
pears to have kept so far as possible the stretch of shore
to the eastward under the guns of some of his ships, but
it could not have been an easy matter with the sailing
craft of that day to remain off a lee shore at times of high
wind and with a strong westerly current, ready night and
day to fire upon a small strip of sand overgrown with man/
groves.

In his criticism of the land operations under General
Wentworth, Admiral Vernon, somewhat overbearing by
nature, seems to have been to some extent unjust, and
that he clearly underestimated the strength of San Lázaro
is evident from letters which he wrote at the time. It
seems doubtful whether in attacking San Lázaro, its weak/
est and most approachable side was accurately determined
in advance; but whether this was so or not, General Went/
worth decided that without effecting a breach an attack
would be impracticable, and much time was consumed in
attempting to raise a battery for the purpose, as well as
in correspondence with Admiral Vernon, respecting the
use of the vessels of the fleet for effecting the breach.
During this time the bulk of the American colonial troops
had been left on the ships, their usefulness being doubted,
more particularly because a large proportion of them were

believed to be Papists; by direction of General Went⁄worth these were landed on the sixth of April, and after⁄wards are credited by the land officers to have rendered gallant services.

On the ninth of April, pressed on the one side by the reproaches of Admiral Vernon for the long delays, and threatened day by day with a lessening power of attack due to the rapidly increasing sickness among his troops, General Wentworth, with the consent of a council of war of the land officers, attempted to carry San Lázaro by storm. The attack was intended to be by night, but owing either to the trickery of native guides, or to badly formed plans on the part of General Wentworth, the attack was begun upon the almost precipitous southern side of the fortress, with scaling ladders of insufficient length. This unfortunate error served to warn the Spanish troops, and the real attack hardly began before the broiling hot tropi⁄cal sun shone relentlessly upon the attacking forces. With a bravery deserving better guidance the troops stood their ground, enduring for hours the terrible fire from above their heads and the burning rays of the sun; but the ram⁄parts were not carried, and finally the troops were forced to retire leaving, it is said, half their number either dead or wounded at the foot of the walls of the fortress. At a council of war of the naval commanders (Vernon, Ogle, and Lestock) on the twelfth of April, it was recommended that in view of the land forces having been unable to erect a battery for effecting a breach in the walls of San Lázaro, and their having failed to storm it otherwise, and also in view of the great sickness prevailing, that "it will be for "the King's service to desist from the enterprise as im/ "practicable." At a council of war of the land officers on the thirteenth of April, the blame for the failure to carry San Lázaro was attributed to the failure of the fleet to adequately co/operate; but the failure of the under/ taking was admitted and definite plans for the embarka/ tion of the troops were suggested. On the fifteenth the stores were taken on board the ships, and on the day fol/ lowing the troops, sadly reduced in numbers and many very ill, were re/embarked. So great were the losses to the troops through disease and battle that not over one third of the land troops appear to have returned with the fleet to Jamaica.

For about a fortnight after the troops were re/embarked, the Admiral kept the fighting vessels employed in de/ stroying the forts and batteries, the structural strength of some of which, particularly of Castillo Grande, appears to have been so great as to have made the work both dif/ ficult and tedious. Also during the interval before sailing an arrangement was made, by means of courteous letters exchanged under flags of truce between the Admiral and the Viceroy, for an exchange of prisoners. On the twenty/ fourth of April, at a general council of war, it was de/ termined to sail for Jamaica as soon as possible, and by

the eighth of May, 1741, the great fleet had left Carta⁄
gena, having, it is true, rendered useless the defences of
the harbour and destroyed six heavy ships and some minor
craft, but having failed to enter the city or to obtain any
substantial booty.

The earlier successes of Vernon made the news of his
failure all the more distressing to the English people, and
the expedition and the causes leading to its failure played
a not unimportant part in English politics for some time.
Unhappily the first despatches to reach England indicated
a repetition of the success at Puerto Bello; premature
celebrations of victory took place and more medals were
struck. For much of the blame put upon Vernon for the
ineffectiveness of the Cartagena expedition Smollett is
responsible. As a surgeon's mate he had accompanied the
fleet and undoubtedly his personal experiences were not
agreeable. Both as a historian and in "Roderick Random"
Smollett shows that his views were coloured by his own
personal relation to the events. Wentworth showed him⁄
self incompetent both in preparation and in performance
and lacking in the qualities of decision and resourcefulness.
Vernon, on the other hand, was an apostle of efficiency;
his real place, however, was in command at sea, and to
some extent he must share the blame for the failure of
the expedition to realize its full purpose. Vernon realized
the importance of sea⁄power, and in one of his official
letters says that he is "strongly convinced that preserv⁄

"ing a superiority at sea is the best security for His Maj-
"esty's Government, as well as of the trade and prosper-
"ity of this Kingdom."

Vernon was a strong advocate of the more humane
treatment of seamen, and in spite of the fact that he
caused their ration of spirits to be diluted, retained their
affection. His popular name of "Old Grog" came from
his habit of wearing grograin breeches; one of his reforms
was to have the rum which was served the fleet regularly
before noon each day diluted with a goodly proportion of
water, a mixture which was thenceforth called "grog."

CHAPTER VI

LORD RODNEY

THE failure of Admiral Vernon at Cartagena contributed to the downfall of Walpole, but neither the latter's retirement nor the lack of success in the attack upon
the Spanish colonies changed the policy of England. The
possession of the West Indies was of too great strategic
and commercial benefit to its possessor for the struggle
for the control of the Caribbean Sea not to continue for
the remainder of the eighteenth century an important
factor in the quarrels for European supremacy. The jeal-
ousies of the English and French settlers in the American colonies served to add fresh causes of trouble between England and France, and for a time the scene of
active hostilities moved northward; English troops were
sent out to assist the colonists against the aggressions of
the French.

In Europe the restless peace following the Treaty of
Aix-la-Chapelle did not weaken the bonds of the family
compact of the House of Bourbon, which kept France
and Spain united against England, and these powers attracted to their support both Austria and Russia. Prussia
alone was in alliance with England when the Seven Years'
War began in 1756.

In the West Indies valuable islands were owned by both France and Spain, and the latter was still in full enjoyment of the rich fortified ports on the mainland.

At this time there was growing up in the naval service of Great Britain a naval officer destined to be one of the great admirals of the English navy, and to exercise the most far-reaching influence on the history of the Caribbean Sea.

George Brydges Rodney was baptised on the thirteenth of February, 1719. He came of a Somersetshire family of some distinction and considerable antiquity. While little more than a child he was sent to Harrow School, which he left at the age of twelve to serve six years with the fleet on the Newfoundland station. At the age of twenty-one he was made lieutenant, and served successively in four ships in the Mediterranean. There appears to be no doubt that, as was not unusual at the time, the high connections of George Rodney contributed to his rapid advancement, although it is equally true that even in his early career he showed marked professional ability. In 1742, at the age of twenty-four, while serving under Admiral Mathews in the Mediterranean, he was given command of the "Plymouth," of sixty guns, as acting post-captain, to which rank he was confirmed by the Admiralty upon his return to England conveying three hundred merchant ships from Lisbon. This service, which was so well performed that it earned for him some public notice, made his subsequent appointments to command conceivably a reward of merit, although it is probable that the exertions of his kinsmen were still needed in his behalf to give him the opportunities for which his abil/ ities fitted him. One appointment followed another for several years, during which, when in command of the "Ludlow Castle," he captured the "St. Malves" priva/ teer, and did efficient work in the transport and despatch service during the war with Scotland.

In the summer of 1747, in the "Eagle," of sixty guns, he joined a small squadron which successfully intercepted a homeward/bound French fleet from Santo Domingo, capturing forty/eight merchantmen of an aggregate bur/ then of over eleven thousand tons, manned by upwards of twelve thousand men, and richly laden with sugar, indigo, coffee, and other West/Indian products. The oc/ casional opportunity to capture fleets of rich merchant vessels made "commerce destroying" a particularly lu/ crative if not otherwise notable service in the days of Hawke, Vernon, and Rodney.

Later in the same year the "Eagle," still under the command of Captain Rodney, formed part of the squad/ ron of fourteen ships which, under Rear/Admiral Hawke, engaged the French fleet under Admiral L'Etenduère off Finisterre. In this engagement, in which six French ships of from fifty to seventy/four guns were captured, after a spirited resistance which permitted their convoy

LORD RODNEY
After Sir Joshua Reynolds

to escape, Captain Rodney was distinguished for gallantry. Upon his return to England, which did not take place until after a successful engagement with a Spanish fleet, he was presented to the King, who received him most graciously.

In 1748, exhausted by years of continuous war, the powers were all desirous for peace. At Aix-la-Chapelle, April 30, 1748, a treaty was signed by England, France, and Holland, and later in the same year by the other belligerent powers. Little had been accomplished by the long war, and the result of the treaty was, with some not very important exceptions, to re-establish the status before the war. A peace so unsatisfactory could not be enduring. The frequent collisions between the English and French colonists in North America brought about a conflict which was inevitable. Finally actual war was in progress, although nominal peace existed between England and France until 1756.

In 1749, Rodney had been appointed Governor and Commander-in-Chief at Newfoundland, a position which developed his political sagacity. His selection for the post by his friend the Earl of Sandwich, then First Lord of the Admiralty, appears to have been because of his known qualities of professional ability and discretion. In 1752, he returned to England, obtained a seat in Parliament, and saw no further active service until the outbreak of war, when he accompanied the Rochefort expedition

under Hawke. In command of the "Dublin" he was attached to the squadron under Admiral Boscawen, which
successfully attacked Louisburg and Cape Breton Island
early in 1758. In May, 1759, Rodney, then forty years
of age, was promoted to the rank of Rear-Admiral, and
given the command of a small squadron sent to bombard
Havre. In 1761, Rodney was appointed to the Leeward
Islands station, with headquarters at Barbadoes, and near
the close of that year took his post in those waters which
were to give him his most enduring title to fame. His
instructions were to attack the French island of Martinique, and troops, under command of Major-General
Monckton, to assist him in the operations, were sent to
him from New York in December.

Admiral Rodney had gone out to his new post with
four ships, three bomb-ketches and a sloop, joining at
Barbadoes a squadron under Sir James Douglas, who, assisted by troops under Lord Rollo, had taken the island
of Dominica. With the ships of the two squadrons, accompanied by the land troops, Admiral Rodney arrived
off Martinique on the seventh of January, 1762. The following day, the forts within range having been silenced
by gun-fire from the ships, the fleet anchored in the Bay
of St. Pierre. One ship, the "Raisonnable," was lost on a
reef through the ignorance of the pilot, during this
operation. Having thus secured a good harbour and landing-place as a base, joint operations of the troops and

ships were conducted with commendable promptness and regularity. Two brigades, under protection of a small squadron, were landed in the Bay of Petit Ance, and the batteries at Grand and St. Anne's Bay were destroyed by fire from the ships.

On the sixteenth, by agreement between the Admiral and General Monckton, the ships silenced the batteries commanding the coast between Point Negro and the Cas de Pilote, and General Monckton, with the whole re-mainder of his troops, was landed without accident by a little after daylight the next morning. With the troops were landed about nine hundred marines, who rendered the most effective help in the subsequent operations. The strength of the resistance offered and the mountain-ous nature of the country made the progress of the land expedition slow, partly no doubt owing to the difficulties met in transporting the heavy ship mortars and cannon any considerable distance from the sea. By the sixteenth of February, however, the French troops had capitulated and the British were in full possession of the island. In Fort Royal Bay the fleet had seized fourteen French pri-vateers, and under the terms of the capitulation all others in the various ports of the island were to be turned over to Admiral Rodney. The harmony which subsisted be-tween Admiral Rodney and General Monckton, and the consequent effectual aid rendered by each arm of the service to the other, contributed in no small degree to the success of this expedition and the speed and smooth⁄ness with which the operations were conducted, and is in sharp contrast to the unfortunate disputes which con⁄tributed to the failure of the Vernon expedition. Admiral Rodney, in his report to the Admiralty, wrote as follows: "It gives me the sincerest satisfaction that I can assure "their Lordships the most perfect harmony has subsisted "between the navy and army, each vying in the most "friendly manner which should serve ‚His Majesty and "their country best." General Monckton expressed him⁄self in a similar way in his official despatches.

From Martinique Admiral Rodney sent a squadron of six vessels to Santa Lucia, the Governor of which, being urged by the inhabitants not to offer resistance, accepted the terms of capitulation offered and surrendered the is⁄land at once. On the fifth of March, the island of Gre⁄nada surrendered without opposition to Commodore Swanton, on the same terms of capitulation accepted by the Governor of Santa Lucia. The terms provided for the peaceful withdrawal and return to France of all troops upon these islands.

While at Martinique, Admiral Rodney received im⁄portant despatches by three separate frigates, which by a strange coincidence arrived together on the same day, the fifth of March. These despatches advised him of the De⁄claration of War against Spain — news then two months old — and of the escape from Brest of a French squadron of seven ships-of-the-line, frigates, and two thousand troops. Shortly afterwards he received an urgent call for help from the Governor and senior naval officer at Jamaica, which island was expecting an attack from the united French and Spanish forces. The situation was one calling for the qualities which Rodney had shown himself to possess. His action was prompt and resolute. Concentrating his greatest strength at Martinique, the probable point of attack of the French fleet, and sending out lookout ships the length of the Windward Islands, he prepared to furnish adequate succour to Jamaica if the Brest fleet should pass by the Windward Islands and go on to the west toward Jamaica and Santo Domingo. On the ninth of March, two of the lookout ships brought word that the French squadron, of thirteen sail in all, had been sighted some fifteen miles to windward of the island. Admiral Rodney at once put to sea with the ships he had retained at Martinique (six ships-of-the-line and ten frigates), but owing to calms and to the fact that the French admiral had altered the course of his squadron when he discovered Martinique to have been taken by the British, the French fleet was not sighted. With commendable promptness he prepared to sail for Jamaica with all the ships at his disposal, but just after sailing he received further despatches from England ordering him to concentrate a powerful force at his own station for the prosecution of an important secret expedition.

Confronted by this serious situation, he took the re/sponsibility, which a man of lesser strength and profes/sional experience might have failed to take, of exercising his general authority and discretion in the interpretation of the orders which the unhappy situation of Jamaica de/manded. He consequently sent Sir James Douglas, with a large re/enforcement of ships, to Jamaica, and returned himself with the remainder to Martinique. In his letter to the Admiralty explaining his purpose of relieving Ja/maica, he expressed himself with characteristic dignity and directness: "I flatter myself their Lordships will not "be displeased with me if I take the liberty to construe "my instructions in such a manner as to think myself au/"thorized and obliged to succour any of His Majesty's "colonies that may be in danger." With the added strength of the ten ships/of/the/line sent to Jamaica, the force there consisted of seventeen ships/of/the/line and thirteen frigates. It is certainly an evidence of the high qualities of Admiral Rodney that, disappointed as he was by the receipt of the secret despatches, which advised him that all plans must be subordinated to an expedition under command of Admiral Sir George Pocock and Lord Albemarle, with Havana as its objective point, he at once took the action necessary to best protect the interests under his charge, and at the same time arranged to co/operate to the fullest extent practicable in an expedition for which credit would go to others.

The vessels of his own squadron he ordered to rendez⁄
vous in Fort Royal Bay, Martinique, and despatched a
frigate to meet Sir George Pocock and advise him of the
fact. He also had taken the precaution to instruct Sir
James Douglas to despatch a frigate from Jamaica to meet
Admiral Pocock and to give him the latest intelligence.

At Martinique, Rodney, with his greatly depleted
squadron, hastened to get everything in readiness against
the arrival of Sir George Pocock and Lord Albemarle.
The troops which could be spared from General Monck⁄
ton's command were embarked on transports several days
before the arrival from England on the twenty⁄sixth of
April, 1762, of Sir George Pocock with the new forces.
Unhappily at this time Admiral Rodney was taken very
ill with bilious fever, and was obliged to be taken on
shore at St. Pierre. The preparations necessary for water⁄
ing the fleet and in other matters required until the sixth
of May, when the men⁄of⁄war and transports under com⁄
mand of Sir George Pocock sailed, a meeting⁄place for a
convoy with troops from Jamaica having been arranged.

The Leeward Islands station, under Rodney, was now
left in a very weakened state. The detachment of so
many vessels and troops left a small force with which to
protect the chain of islands which had been taken by
Rodney, and that he felt keen anxiety is shown by his
despatches to the Admiralty written at the time. Not⁄
withstanding the bad state of his health, Rodney dealt

vigorously with all the annoying problems of his station. Owing to the precautions taken and to the prestige he and his ships had acquired, no event of importance disturbed the Leeward Islands station during the remainder of the Seven Years' War. Admiral Pocock effected a junction with the Jamaica re/enforcement late in May, and pro/ ceeded through the Bahama Channel on the north side of Cuba, a passage then not carefully charted, and ap/ peared before Havana with his great fleet about the twen/ tieth of June. After a prolonged siege of forty days, Moro Castle was taken on the thirtieth of July. About a fort/ night later, Havana surrendered. The capture included some dozen ships/of/the/line and nearly fifteen million dollars' worth of goods and money. With the Lesser An/ tilles in the grasp of Rodney and Havana surrendered to Pocock, Cartagena was the only fortified naval base of consequence left to Spain in the West Indies not infested with British ships.

In October of the same year, Manila was captured by the British and a ransom of four million dollars paid. Spain suffered at the same time other severe losses through the capture of several homeward/bound treasure ships. In September, peace was declared and made effective by a treaty signed on the tenth of February, 1763. The treaty, so far as it related to the West Indies, gave Gre/ nada, the Grenadines, Dominica, St. Vincent, and Tobago to Great Britain. Guadeloupe, Martinique, and St. Lucie were restored to France (the entire province of Canada and part of Louisiana being ceded to the English). Spain gave up to England all that she possessed on the conti/ nent of North America to the east of the Mississippi River, and Havana was restored to Spain.

In October, 1762, Admiral Rodney was made Vice/ Admiral of the Blue. He returned to England in August, 1763, and in January of the next year was made a Baro/ net. For five years, from December, 1765, he served as Governor of the Royal Hospital at Greenwich. In 1770, he was made Vice/Admiral of the White, and in 1771, Vice/Admiral of the Red. In January, 1771, he was ap/ pointed Commander/in/Chief at Jamaica. In this position he was unable to retain, somewhat to his chagrin, as he appears to have needed the additional income to relieve his pecuniary embarrassments, his position as Governor of the Hospital.

On the twenty/fourth of July, with a squadron of six ships, he arrived at his new post, Port Royal, Jamaica, find/ ing there six vessels under Commodore Mackenzie. With the promptness and decision which was always a charac/ teristic of Rodney, he had not been in command of the station a fortnight before he had put surveying parties at work planning a proper watering/place, afterwards per/ fected, for the vessels of the fleet at Rock Fort, to replace the tedious method of boat carriage then employed. Po/ litical ability and tactfulness of a high order were needed in the commander charged with keeping the peace and upholding the dignity of the British flag in those waters at this time, and Rodney's demonstrated ability in this direction undoubtedly was a convincing reason for his selection. The peace concluded at the end of 1762 had not served to establish free commercial relations between the Spanish and British colonies, and regulations of the most exclusive and irritating nature were imposed at all the Spanish ports in the Caribbean Sea. As was natural, smuggling continued and increased. Jamaica, surrounded by a circle of Spanish ports, became the centre of an il/ licit trade. To facilitate trade relations Jamaica established several free ports, which brought about increased vigi/ lance on the part of the Spanish coast guards. This at/ tempted protection of the Spanish ports was chiefly by small vessels called "guarda/costas." A profitable busi/ ness was done by both English and French traders in eluding these vessels and transporting goods to and from Jamaica, which served as a market/place for the trade.

Shortly after Rodney's arrival in Jamaica, the island, particularly the towns of Kingston and Port Royal, were damaged by an earthquake, the most severe that had been experienced since the great one of 1692, but the fleet met with no great injury. Embarrassed as he was by con/ ditions ripe for war, Rodney appears to have used a firm and strong hand in the interests of peace. His letter, sent by a frigate to the Governor of Cartagena after two Span/

ish guarda⁄costas had overhauled and taken into Carta⁄
gena harbour the British man⁄of⁄war " Hawke," is worthy
of quotation, as illustrating both the temper of the times
and the discretion with which Rodney dealt with a most
difficult situation:

" Princess Amelia, Jamaica,
"September 3d, 1771.

" To the Governor of Carthagena.

"I have the honour to acquaint your Excellency, that
"his Britanic Majesty has been pleased to confer on me
"the command of his squadron on this station, and to as⁄
"sure you that while I am protecting his Majesty's terri⁄
"tories, and the trade of his subjects, I shall be truly
"solicitous to maintain a friendly correspondence with
"your Excellency, and with the rest of his Catholic
" Majesty's governors in America.

" With such a disposition, judge, Sir, what must have
"been my astonishment to hear, on my arrival, that two
"guarda⁄costas, under the pretended sanction of your
" Excellency's and the Commodore's orders, had forced
"his Majesty's schooner, the Hawke, into Carthagena,
"after they were told, and knew whose commission the
"commander of her had the honour to bear.

"I am moreover informed, that one of the Commo⁄
"dore's lieutenants, acquainted the commander of the
"schooner, on her dismission from the port of Cartha⁄
" gena, that she might go, but that if either the schooner,

"or any other of his Britanic Majesty's ships were after-
"wards found within twelve leagues of that coast, they
"should be taken and their crews imprisoned.

" As your Excellency, I doubt not, is equally disposed
" with myself to support the harmony which so happily
" subsists between the two crowns, I cannot be persuaded
" that you have given the least countenance to these acts
"of violence.

"The officer who had dishonoured his King's colours
" by a tame submission to this insult has been already dis-
"missed the service ; and I have the fullest confidence
"that your Excellency will, on your part, immediately
"order the officers that have treated with such indignity
"the British flag to be called to the strictest account, and
"confirm the opinion I would willingly entertain of the
"impossibility of such a menace being sent by the Com-
"modore, or any officer of rank, who wishes to preserve
"the general tranquillity.

"I have ordered the captain by whom I send this to
"wait your Excellency's answer."

In 1774, when Rodney's appointment expired, he endeavoured unsuccessfully to get the appointment as Governor of Jamaica or of some other colony. Upon his
return to England in September of that year, financial
troubles, from which his service had temporarily freed
him, began again. To escape these embarrassments he

took up his residence in France, to await a time when renewed employment would enable him to meet his cred, itors. It is not improbable that the almost continued dis, tressed condition of his personal affairs, accounts to some extent for the opposition which from time to time in his career met his efforts for advancement, in spite of his ad, mittedly high professional ability. Until early in 1778, Rodney remained in France, fretting under the lack of recognition, when Howe was sent to America in 1776, and later, when with war under way with the American colonies, his juniors were sent out in command of the North,American and West,Indian stations. The condi, tions, however, soon made his employment almost a ne, cessity. Through the kindly aid of a French gentleman who had become his friend, and with the help of friends in England, his debts were adjusted,* and on the first of October, 1779, he was again appointed to the command of the Leeward Islands station. War with the American colonies had begun in 1776, the French had declared war in 1778, and Spain in 1779. In the West Indies, Grenada had been lost to the British. The task to which Rodney was put was therefore not an easy one.

* L'amiral Rodney s'y trouvait alors retenu pour des dettes qu'il ne pouvait solder. Un jour qu'il dînait chez le Maréchal de Biron, il traita avec dédain les succès des marins français, disant que s'il était libre, il en aurait bientôt raison. Le Maréchal paya aussitôt ses dettes : "partez, Monsieur," lui dit-il ; "allez essayer de remplir vos promesses ; les Français ne veulent "pas se prévaloir des obstacles qui vous empêchent de les accomplir."— V. Duruy's *Histoire de France.*

On the twenty-ninth of December, 1779, he sailed from Plymouth with twenty-one ships-of-the-line, a small portion only of which was to continue with him to the West Indies, the bulk of the force being assigned to him for the purpose of attempting the relief of Gibraltar, the long siege of which had then begun. With the fleet were the usual proportion of frigates and a large number of store and troop ships, as well as merchantmen, many of the latter being bound for the West Indies and parting company with the fleet about a week after it sailed. The good fortune which Rodney needed in order to create anew the enthusiasm which his successes had gained for him in the previous war, by a happy chance came quickly. On the eighth of January, 1780, a Spanish convoy of twenty-two sail was sighted, and found to be made up of seven ships-of-war and the remainder merchantmen loaded with naval stores and provisions. Admiral Rodney at once gave chase and the whole were taken. The seven ships-of-war carried a total of two hundred and six guns and twelve hundred and ninety-three men, the largest being the "Guipuscuano," of sixty-four guns and five hundred and fifty men. Twelve of the convoy, loaded with flour and wheat, were sent on with the other British ships to carry provisions to the garrison at Gibraltar. The balance, containing naval stores, were despatched under convoy to England. The "Guipuscuano" was commissioned, officered, manned, and named the "Prince

"William," in honour of the Prince (afterwards King Wil/
liam IV) who was a midshipman with the fleet.

Intelligence that a Spanish squadron, said to consist
of fourteen ships/of/the/line, was cruising off Cape St. Vin/
cent, had reached Admiral Rodney, and by his orders the
fleet kept in readiness for battle as the Cape was ap/
proached. On the afternoon of the sixteenth of January,
a few hours after passing the Cape, the Spanish fleet was
sighted in the south/east quarter. Owing to the lateness
of the day and the necessity for prompt action, Rodney
gave up what had been his first intention to form a
line of battle abreast, and made the signal for a general
chase. At four o'clock the enemy were engaged; within
less than an hour the magazines of one of the Spanish
line/of/battle ships were exploded, destroying the ship,
and at six one of their ships struck. The engagement
continued until two o'clock the next morning. The tem/
pestuous weather and nearness of a dangerous lee shore
prevented the continuance of the engagement, and six of
the Spanish ships escaped, several in badly damaged con/
dition. Four of the ships, carrying seventy to eighty guns,
were taken and sent into Gibraltar; two others struck,
but were lost on the shoals; one was blown up in action.

Within less than three weeks of leaving England,
Rodney, by good fortune and efficient work, had, as Lord
Sandwich in his letter of congratulation to him wrote,
"taken more line/of/battle ships than had been cap/

"tured in any one action in either of the two last preced-
"ing wars." The thanks of both Houses of Parliament
were voted to Admiral Rodney, the motion in the House
of Lords being made by Lord Sandwich himself, who
continued as First Lord of the Admiralty.

On the thirteenth of February, Rodney left Gibraltar
for the West Indies, sailing with his fleet directly for
Barbadoes. At this time the French had a strong fleet at
Fort Royal Bay, Martinique, under the command of one
of their most able commanders, Admiral de Guichen.
The movements of this fleet were closely watched by ships
stationed by Rodney for the purpose, and when, on the
fifteenth of April, de Guichen sailed from Martinique
with a convoy bound for Santo Domingo, Rodney followed instantly with his fleet, which he had kept ready
to pursue or engage the French fleet. Late on the sixteenth, the fleets were within sight of one another. The
fleet under de Guichen consisted of twenty-three ships-of-
the-line, having a total of fifteen hundred and fifty guns,
six frigates, one lugger, and a cutter. Rodney had under
his command twenty ships-of-the-line, having a total of
thirteen hundred and ninety guns, and five frigates. On
the seventeenth, the two fleets were in approximately
parallel lines, headed in opposite directions, with the
British in the windward position. Both commanders were
possessed of high tactical skill, and the record of the prolonged engagement of these two fleets is of greater tech-

nical than historical interest. Rodney's intention is clearly
described in the words of his own report: "At forty⁄six
"minutes after six I gave notice that intention was to at⁄
"tack the enemy's rear with my whole force, which sig⁄
"nal was answered by every ship in the fleet." Appar⁄
ently this intention was discovered by de Guichen in
time to permit him to strengthen his threatened rear,
and the resulting engagement by a change in orders
became more nearly a "ship⁄to⁄ship" battle. Owing to
an unfortunate misunderstanding of the orders given,
a number of the ships of Rodney's fleet, by attacking
the wrong vessels of the French fleet, extended and
weakened the British line, instead of concentrating it as
Rodney had carefully planned. This failure to properly
interpret and obey his instructions brought upon the
offenders the most severe treatment by the Admiral,
whose indignation is fittingly expressed in the words
of his despatch to the Admiralty: "It is with con⁄
"cern inexpressible, mixed with indignation, that the
"duty I owe my Sovereign and country obliges me to
"acquaint their Lordships that, during the action with
"the French fleet on the 17th instant, and his Majesty's,
"the British flag was not properly supported." The crit⁄
ics of Rodney blame him for making his intentions clear.

Notwithstanding that the hoped⁄for results were not
obtained in this action, Rodney had personally shown the
greatest skill and courage, and had the satisfaction to know

that he had badly damaged a French fleet his superior in strength, and whose gallant commander, having been obliged to adopt defensive rather than offensive tactics, had, after being pursued for three days, taken refuge at Guadeloupe. Of Admiral de Guichen, Rodney reports "that the French Admiral, who appeared to me to be a "brave and gallant officer, had the honour to be nobly "supported during the whole action."

Expecting that the French fleet would attempt to re/gain Martinique, Admiral Rodney kept a close watch upon its movements, with a view of intercepting it and forcing another engagement. On the nineteenth of May, both of the fleets were again at sea and in sight of one another. That the French admiral endeavoured to avoid action was due not to a lack of courage, but to the instruc/tions from his Government, which clearly directed him not to compromise the safety of his fleet. From the ninth to the twenty/second, the two fleets manœuvred at vary/ing distances, the French ships being aided in their defen/sive tactics by superior speed. During this prolonged pe/riod of sustained exertion and vigilance, advantage was taken of every possible opportunity for a successful attack, but with the exception of partial engagements on the fifteenth to nineteenth, Admiral de Guichen was able to skilfully elude the attempts. On the fifteenth, consider/able damage was done to the rear of the French fleet by the van of the British fleet, and on the nineteenth, dam/

age was again inflicted. On the twenty-first, the French fleet finally escaped and in somewhat shattered condition reached Martinique. Rodney proceeded to Barbadoes to land his wounded and to repair his damaged ships.

At this time he received intelligence of the sailing of a Spanish fleet of about twenty ships-of-the-line from Cadiz on the twenty-eighth of April, and stationed a line of frigates to windward to give timely notice of its approach. Early in May (1780), a Spanish fleet of some two hun-dred sail was reported to be about one hundred and fifty miles to windward of Martinique. Rodney, although im-mediately setting sail, succeeded in sighting three ships only, two of which being taken proved to be part of the convoy from Cadiz, one with goods and the other with troops. The Spanish fleet, with the remainder of its large convoy, had successfully passed to leeward.

Rodney was now troubled by the probability of the French and Spanish fleets forming a junction, which was in fact accomplished in July (1780). He had been disap-pointed in not receiving expected re-enforcements from the American station, and his own fleet could not safely attempt to cover the whole West-Indian waters. Before leaving England, Rodney had arranged with Lord Sand-wich that during the winter months the fleet under Ad-miral Arbuthnot, operating against the rebellious Amer-ican colonies, should join the West-Indian fleet, and that later, when the hurricane season made the West Indies

unsafe, the combined fleet should work together in Amer/
ican waters. Owing to a disaster to the vessel carrying the
despatches to Arbuthnot, the orders were received by him
too late.

Expecting that de Guichen would endeavour to join
the French fleet under de Ternay, which had been sent
by France to the aid of the American colonists, Rodney
again had the courage to construe his duty to be to protect
the King's interests wherever occasion demanded. He
arranged as best he could for the security of his own sta/
tion, and proceeded with a good portion of his fleet to
New York, where he arrived off Sandy Hook the four/
teenth of September, 1780. With the incidents of this
visit to American waters, which were not particularly
eventful, it is not the purpose of this account to deal, as
the expedition had little bearing on events in the Carib/
bean Sea. Rodney, as his superior in command, was not
welcomed by Arbuthnot, but Rodney appears to have
borne himself with his customary dignity, and to have
exercised his authority in more than a nominal capacity.
Beyond the frequent capture of privateers, little of conse/
quence was accomplished by Rodney's fleet by this visit
to American waters. The French fleet at Newport it was
not found expedient to attack at that place, and de Gui/
chen had returned directly to France instead of joining de
Ternay in America. In December, 1780, Rodney returned
to the West Indies with a fleet of fifteen ships, in time to

be of help to the islands, which were suffering from the effects of a disastrous hurricane.

At this time the united forces of France, Spain, and America, against which Great Britain was contending, received the tacit support of a formidable confederacy, called the "Armed Neutrality," which included Russia, Denmark, Sweden, and Holland. Of these countries Holland in particular gave encouragement to the American colonies and offence to Great Britain when, in the words of Lord North, its Government "suffered Paul Jones, a "Scotchman and a pirate, acting without any legal au "thority from any acknowledged government, to bring " British ships into their ports and to refit there." The capture of an American packet, the "Mercury," having on board an agent of the American Congress on an embassy to Holland, with the draft of a treaty of amity and commerce between the two republics, brought the already strained relations to the breaking point, and war was declared by Great Britain against Holland. Despatches notifying him of this reached Rodney on the twenty-seventh of January, 1781, at Barbadoes, and ordered him to at once attack the Dutch West Indies and shipping. The Dutch and other merchants of St. Eustatius and St. Martin had profited largely by the trade made possible by their position of neutrality, and these islands had become a storehouse for the accumulation of the goods of the traders of all nationalities. In the instructions sent out to Rodney, the object of attack first designated was St. Eustatius, and not a moment's time was lost by the Admiral and General Vaughan in putting the command into execution. On the thirtieth of January, the British fleet sailed from Santa Lucia to attack St. Eustatius, leaving a squadron under Rear-Admiral Drake to watch the small squadron of French ships still remaining in the Bay of Fort Royal, Martinique. In January, Rodney had been re-enforced by a squadron of eight ships-of-the-line under Rear-Admiral Sir Samuel Hood, who had been sent out to serve as his second in command, and this squadron was sent to surround the bay of St. Eustatius to prevent the escape of any vessels from the port. On the third of February, Rodney, with the remainder of the fleet and the troops under General Vaughan, arrived in the bay. Having made this display of force, the Admiral and General joined in a summons for the "instant surrender of the Island of St. Eustatius "and its dependencies, with everything in and belonging "thereto." The Dutch Governor at once complied with the demand, which was shortly followed by the uncon-ditional surrender of the islands of St. Martin and Saba.

The value of this capture was enormous; upwards of one hundred and fifty ships of all classes were taken, in-cluding one man-of-war of thirty-eight guns and three hundred men, and five of from fourteen to twenty-six guns each, all equipped and ready for immediate service. The capture was followed by the seizure of several additional ships outward/bound with naval stores, and by the capture of a Dutch convoy of some thirty richly laden merchant ships, which had left St. Eustatius a day or two before its surrender. This convoy alone was valued at more than half a million sterling, and the value of the whole property seized was estimated by Rodney at be/tween two and three millions sterling.

Attacks upon the island of Curaçao and upon Surinam were now planned, but owing to intelligence, which subsequently proved to be erroneous, that a French squad/ron of eight or ten ships/of/the/line were headed for the Caribbean Sea, a change of plans was made expedient, and the attacks were not made. During the early part of March, however, the Dutch colonies of Demerara and Essequibo surrendered, together with the French island of St. Bartholomew. All the Leeward Islands thus passed into British hands.

To meet this reported French fleet Rodney detached Rear/Admiral Hood with seventeen ships/of/the/line to watch for the enemy to windward of Martinique, a position which at the end of a month, contrary to the advice of Hood, he ordered changed to the leeward of the island, in order to blockade Fort Royal harbour, in which were still four French ships/of/the/line. The ex/pected French fleet never arrived, but on the twenty/second of March (1781), more than five weeks after Hood had begun his wearisome watching, a French fleet of twenty ships-of-the-line did actually sail from Brest for Martinique, under Admiral the Comte de Grasse. On the twenty-eighth of April, Hood sighted this fleet; but on account of his position to leeward he was unable to prevent the junction with it of the four ships from Fort Royal, which made the total strength of de Grasse twenty-four ships-of-the-line. Against this formidable fleet were but eighteen ships under Hood, the French fleet also having the advantage of the weather-gage.

Either from fear for the safety of his convoy, which was large, or for some other unaccountable reason, de Grasse did not make the most of his advantageous posi-tion to force an engagement, and Hood, having good reason to believe an engagement unwise, successfully withdrew his squadron, and joined Rodney on the elev-enth of May, near Antigua.

Rodney has been blamed for the apparent tactical blunder in not having had his fleet concentrated under his own personal command in a good strategic position to have met de Grasse with sufficient force upon his ar-rival. It is difficult, however, to criticise justly acts which were governed by so many doubtful factors at the time. Rodney believed it of paramount importance to guard from attack the captures he had already made, the ma-terial value of which undoubtedly weighed too heavily in his judgment. As it turned out, the course he pursued made impossible a successful attack upon de Grasse. That it was of greater importance to destroy the efficiency of the French fleet than to preserve the booty gained in the previous engagements, was not fully realized by Rodney. If the subsequent operations of de Grasse upon the American coast had been rendered impossible, even the surrender of Cornwallis might not so soon have taken place.

De Grasse made an attack upon Santa Lucia, but failed, and shortly afterwards proceeded to Tobago, to which British island he had already sent a small squadron. Rodney, not knowing that de Grasse had followed with his whole fleet to Tobago, had sent for the defence of that place six ships only under Rear-Admiral Drake. In the meantime Rodney had collected his fleet at Barbadoes, and received intelligence there of the movement of the French fleet in time to arrive off Tobago on the fifth of June, three days after the island had surrendered to de Grasse. Early in July, de Grasse, having continued to successfully elude the British fleet, sailed for Haiti, at which place he planned to organize his expedition to the American coast to co-operate with the army under General Washington. He was closely followed by a squadron despatched by Rodney under Hood, which it was expected would be re-enforced by ships from Jamaica. De Grasse, however, made no long delay before sailing with his whole fleet for North America, and displaying his customary adroitness left the West Indies.

Having obtained permission, on account of the state

of his health, to return for a brief visit to England, Rodney gave orders to Hood for the employment of the British fleet on the North-American station during the hurricane months, and sailed for England with a small
detachment and convoy of some one hundred and fifty
sail, arriving on the nineteenth of September,1781. Having to some extent re-established his health by a sojourn
at Bath, he received commands in November to return to
the West Indies, this time as Commander-in-Chief of the
whole West-Indian station. At the same time he was promoted to the high dignity of Vice-Admiral of Great Britain, succeeding Lord Hawke, who died on the seventeenth of October, 1781.

A considerable portion of his time before sailing early
in January, 1782, was given up to the defence by him
of charges made in the House of Commons relative to
alleged improper seizure of goods at St. Eustatius. These
charges chiefly arose from the confiscation of goods belonging, or purporting to belong, to Englishmen residing
on the island at the time of its capture. The taking of
the goods was justified by Rodney on the ground of the
illegal or contraband nature of the trade in which the
owners had been engaged. He also found it necessary to
explain the causes which led to the apparent inactivity
of his forces during the operations of the fleet under de
Grasse, regarding which inactivity charges were also made
in the House of Commons. That he still retained the

confidence of the King and Admiralty is evident from his appointment to a larger area of command and to an in crease in naval rank. In a final note sent to him just be fore his departure, the Earl of Sandwich wrote, "The "fate of the empire is in your hands, and I have no rea "son to wish that it should be in any other."

Advices that the Comte de Grasse, after a drawn battle with the British fleet off the mouth of the Chesapeake and the surrender of Cornwallis, had sailed with his whole fleet to the West Indies, hurried the preparations of Rod ney, who promised to bring "back a present of de Grasse" to the British nation.

With the squadron he had brought out from England he arrived at Barbadoes on the nineteenth of February, 1782, to find a troubled situation which required the full est exercise of his high abilities. Before the return of Hood from the north, St. Eustatius had been recaptured by two French frigates with about three hundred men. The British garrison at St. Kitts was besieged and capitu lated six days before his arrival. The large French fleet under de Grasse, of some thirty three ships of the line, was held back only by the superior tactical ability of Hood, the strength of whose squadron was scarcely two thirds that of the French fleet. Rodney proceeded to Antigua and arranged a junction there, on the twenty fifth of Febru ary, of his squadron with that of Hood, sailing with the united fleet to Santa Lucia, where he arrived on the fifth of March. After an unsuccessful attempt to intercept a fleet of supply ships intended for de Grasse, Rodney col-lected his fleet at Gros Ilet Bay, Santa Lucia, not more than thirty miles from the French fleet, which had reached and anchored at Fort Royal Bay without Rodney being able to bring them to action. At this time the situ-ation was further complicated by the presence of a squad-ron of American privateers which threatened the island of Tortola, for the protection of which Rodney de-spatched four frigates. He also detached a small squadron to attempt the recapture of Montserrat, which island had been taken by the French.

The purpose of de Grasse, who, in addition to his large fleet of ships-of-the-line, had a very considerable convoy of troop-ships with over five thousand troops on board, ammunition vessels, &c., was to join a Spanish fleet at Cap François (now Cape Haitien), Hispaniola. The com-bined fleets, with the troops and artillery, were expected to form a sufficiently strong force to make the capture of Jamaica possible. To prevent the carrying out of this plan, Rodney exerted to the fullest his great capacity and skill. By a chain of frigates within signalling distance of one another, he kept himself in touch with the movements of the French fleet at Fort Royal Bay. On the morning of the eighth of April, de Grasse sailed with thirty-five ships-of-the-line, followed at once by the British fleet of thirty-six ships-of-the-line. At nightfall, Rodney had the

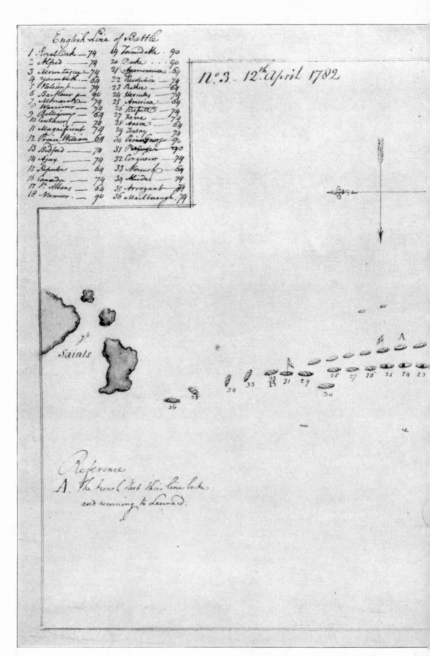

English Line of Battle

1. Royal Oak — 74	19. Formidable — 90
2. Alfred — 74	20. Duke — 90
3. Montague — 74	21. Agamemnon — 64
4. Yarmouth — 64	22. Resolution — 74
5. Valiant — 74	23. Prothee — 64
6. Barfleur — 90	24. Hercules — 74
7. Alcmene — 74	25. America — 64
8. Warrior — 74	26. Russell — 74
9. Bellona — 64	27. Fame — 74
10. Centaur — 74	28. Anson — 64
11. Magnificent — 74	29. Torbay — 74
12. Prince William — 64	30. Prince George — 90
13. Bedford — 74	31. Prince — 90
14. Ajax — 74	32. Conqueror — 74
15. Repulse — 64	33. Nonsuch — 64
16. Canada — 74	34. Medea — 74
17. St. Albans — 64	35. Arrogant — 74
18. Namur — 90	36. Marlborough — 74

N.º 3 — 12ᵗʰ April 1782

Saints

Reference
A. The French Fleet their line broke
and running to Leeward.

PLAN OF ENGAGEMENT OF FLEETS UN

From a

DER RODNEY AND DE GRASSE ON THE 12TH APRIL, 1782

collection of contemporary records

French ships in sight, and at daybreak on the ninth the greater part of the fleet were visible from the decks of the British ships. De Grasse, finding it impossible to avoid an action by superior speed while handicapped by his convoy, signalled it to put into Guadeloupe, which order was promptly obeyed. The British fleet was too close, however, for de Grasse to evade an engagement, and on the ninth several skirmishes took place between the French rear and the British van. On the tenth and eleventh, the pursuit continued, a badly managed or slow ship from the French fleet from time to time dropping back.

Early on the twelfth, the flag-ship of de Grasse collided with one of the largest of his ships-of-the-line, the "Zélé," damaging the latter to an extent which made it necessary to send it into Guadeloupe under tow of a frigate. De Grasse had taken his fleet into the passage between Do- minica and Guadeloupe, which required the ships to beat to windward. Hood, being signalled by Rodney to pursue the "Zélé," did so, which served to draw de Grasse hastily to her support, signalling his fleet to form line-of-battle. The two fleets shortly passed each other in approximately parallel lines in opposite directions, the French fleet to windward, and the conditions unfavour- able for Rodney to force a close action. A fortunate shift of the wind from the east to the south-east served to weaken the French formation, and enabled the British ships to stand in to the French line. This was effectually done, Rodney in his flag-ship the "Formidable," followed by a portion of his fleet, breaking through about the middle of de Grasse's line, separating his fleet into several groups and putting the main body of the British fleet to windward. Feeble breezes and calms during the rest of the day gave added advantage to the windward position obtained by Rodney. At nightfall the "Ville de Paris," the flag-ship of de Grasse, struck. To this capture Hood, who found fault with the failure of Rodney to reap the full benefit of his advantageous position, attributes the lack of taking other ships, as he charges Rodney with having been so overcome with delight at the capture of the flag-ship, that he let the chance slip by of taking "a "dozen better ships in lieu of her."

In an account of this battle written by Sir Gilbert Blane, physician to the fleet, the loss upon the British side was reported to be two hundred and sixty-one killed, and eight hundred and thirty-seven wounded. In addition to the "Ville de Paris," flag-ship, of one hundred and six guns and thirteen hundred men, some six other smaller ships were taken or destroyed. The "Ville de Paris" alone was reported to have had over three hundred killed and wounded men. The total number in the ships lost to the French, which included five of from sixty-four to seventy-four guns, must have been a number of thousands.

The defeated French fleet was scattered and disabled,

but owing to lack of a continuous and sustained attack by the British ships, managed to escape, and in part pro⁄ceeded toward Cap François, where finally some nine⁄teen ships came together. The remainder in due course reached Curaçao.

In spite of the failure to secure the full success which appears to have been so readily within his grasp, Rod⁄ney's victory was far⁄reaching in its results. In its influ⁄ence on the course of events it was the greatest of any naval battle of the war, and it was possibly due to a per⁄ception of this that made Rodney content with a defi⁄nite victory and shrink from the risk of a possible later reverse.

The reports of the battle reached England at a good time. The promptness with which the French fleet was followed from Fort Royal Bay, and the brilliancy of the first attack, together with the capture of the enemy's flag⁄ship and the Comte de Grasse, won great credit for Rodney, although subsequently the events were the basis of an active controversy. He was voted the thanks of Parliament, with an additional pension of two thousand pounds per annum, and made a peer by the King.

Although not actually destroyed, the French fleet was no longer to be feared, and Jamaica was saved. To that island Rodney repaired with his prizes to refit his ships. The Comte de Grasse was taken to Jamaica, and from there on the nineteenth of May despatched to England as a prisoner, but one to whom the most courteous and flattering attention was constantly given.

The fall of the Ministry, which was one of the results of the surrender of Cornwallis, brought about changes in the Government, and Lord Sandwich was succeeded by Lord Keppel as First Lord of the Admiralty. Before the news of his encounter with de Grasse reached England, the new Admiralty had sent out orders displacing Rod-ney and appointing Admiral Pigot to succeed him. When the news arrived, Admiral Pigot had already sailed, and on the twenty-second of July, Admiral Rod-ney left Jamaica, arriving home on the fifteenth of Sep-tember, 1782.

His stay in Jamaica had been marked by many demon-strations of respect and gratitude, and in the following year the governing council, or House of Assembly of the island, voted funds toward erecting a statue of Lord Rod-ney "as a mark of gratitude and veneration for his gal-"lant services, so timely and gloriously performed for "the salvation of the island in particular, as well as the "whole of the British West India islands."

Upon Lord Rodney's return to England, he lived for the greater part of the time with his family in retirement in the country, although occupied to some extent with legal matters growing out of the seizures at St. Eustatius. He continued to be troubled with the gout, which had annoyed him during his later voyages, and on the twenty-

ENGLISH FLEET UNDER RODNEY, HOOD, DRAKE, AND AFFLECK BREAKING THE
LINE OF THE FRENCH FLEET, APRIL 12, 1782

third of May, 1792, he died, at the age of seventy-three. He had been in the navy sixty-two years, about fifty of which had been in commission, an extraordinary period of active service.

The defeat of de Grasse by Rodney practically ended the war for the Bourbons. Later in the same year, Great Britain made a treaty of peace with the United States, which was shortly followed by treaties of peace with the Bourbon powers. The latter had gained little by the war. In America Great Britain had lost the rebellious states, but had increased her prestige and power in the West Indies, a fact from which at the time little comfort was derived. With the dawning of a new century, the Caribbean Sea lost much of its importance as a battle-ground for European quarrels, although the successful wars of the Spanish colonies for independence from Spain made it the arena for many more struggles at both the beginning and end of the nineteenth century.

THE END

PARTIAL LIST OF SOURCES AND BIBLIOGRAPHY

Printed Sources

Historia General de las Indias, by Gonzalo Fernandez de Oviedo y Valdes, 1526 and 1535.

Novus Orbis, ed. by S. Grynæus, Paris, 1532.

Libro Primo della Historia del' Indie Occidentali . . . by Peter Martyr, Venice, 1534.

Libro Ultimo de Summario de Indie, by Peter Martyr, Venice, 1534.

The Decades of the New World, by Peter Martyr, London, 1555.

Historia General de las Indias, by F. Lopez de Gomara, 1552–53.

Breuissima relacion de la destruycion de las Indias, etc., by B. de las Casas, Sevilla, 1552–53.

Primo Volume Delle Navigationi et Viaggi . . . by Giov. B. Ramusio, Venice, 1554. (Second vol. and 3d edition, 1583.)

Historia de Mondo Nuovo, by Girol. Benzoni, Venice, 1565 and 1572.

Historia natural y moral de las Indias, by José de Acosta, Sevilla, 1590.

Americæ, by J. Theo. de Bry, Parts III to VIII, Francofurti, 1592–99.

Historia General de los Hechos de los Castellanos, by A. de Herrera, Madrid, 1601–15.

The English-American, his Travail by Sea & Land; or A New Survey of the West Indies, by Thomas Gage, London, 1648.

A New Voyage & Description of the Isthmus of America, by Lionel Wafer, London, 1699.

Coleccion de los viages y descubrimientos, by Mart. F. de Navarrete, Madrid, 1825–37.

Dampier's Voyages, edited by John Masefield, London, 1906.
The Journals of Columbus, records, etc., included in the various standard editions of the Life of Columbus.

DRAKE

Printed Sources

The Principall Navigations, Voiages and Discoveries of the English Nation, . . . by Richard Hakluyt. London, 1589. (Containing the account by Thomas Cates of Drake's voyage in 1585, the voyage around the world, etc.)

Sir Francis Drake Revived, by Philip Nichols, London, 1626.

Hakluytus Posthumus, or Purchas his Pilgrimes, Contayning . . . Sea Voyages, and Lande Travells, by Englishmen and Others, by Samuel Purchas, London, 1625. (Containing Camden's account of Drake's youth and voyages, the narrative of Peter Carder, etc.)

The World Encompassed by Sir Francis Drake, collected from the notes of Master Francis Fletcher, London, 1652.

Coleccion de Documentos Inéditos relativos al descubrimiento conquista y colonization de las possessiones espanoles en America . . . Madrid, 1864–84.

Drake and the Tudor Navy, by J. S. Corbett, London, 1898.

MORGAN

Printed Sources

Calendar of State Papers, Colonial Series, 1669 *et seq.* Containing:

Journal of Lords of Trade and Plantations.

Extracts from Journal of the Assembly of Jamaica.

Extracts from Minutes of the Council of Jamaica.

Official reports, orders and appointments.

Petitions, libels, affidavits and enquiries.

Letters to and from Sir Henry Morgan, Lord Vaughan, the Earl of Carlisle, Governor Modyford, Francis Mingham and others.

Bucaniers of America, Or, a true Account of the Most remarkable assaults committed of late years upon the Coasts of the West Indies, by John Esquemeling, London, 1684.

Correspondence of the Family of Hatton (vol. 2), Camden Society, 1878.

Buccaneers in the West Indies in the XVII Century, by C. H. Haring (a thesis presented to the Board of Modern History at Oxford in May, 1909), New York, 1910.

Governors of Jamaica, by Frank Cundall, Kingston, 1920.

Manuscripts

"Additional Manuscripts," vols. 11268 and 13964, British Museum.

State Papers (Spain), vols. 57 and 58, Public Record Office, London.

Contemporaneous Minutes in the Council Book of Jamaica, 1672–78.

Coram Rege Roll, King's Bench, No. 2041 m. 526, Easter Term 1, James II (1685). Malthus, Thos. ats. Henry Morgan Knt.

BARON DE POINTIS

Printed Sources

Calendar of State Papers, Colonial Series, 1696–97.

Relation de ce qui c'est fait la Prise de Carthagéne, par le Sieur de Pointis, Bruxelles, 1698.

Relation Fidele de l'Expedition de Cartagena, [Paris,] 1699.

De Pointis Expedition to Cartagena: the Taking of the City by the French, their meeting with Admiral Nevil, etc. (translated from the French). [London,] 1699.

Histoire de l'isle Espagnola ou de S. Dominique écrite particulièrement sur des Memoirs manuscrits du P. Jean Baptiste le Pers . . . Par le P. Pierre François Xavier de Charlevoix, de la Compagnie de Jésus, Paris, 1731.

Account of the Taking of Cartagena by the French and Buccaniers, in the Year 1697, by the Sieur Pointis, Commander in Chief (translated from the French), London, 1740.

Histoire des Flibustiers, de J. W. d'Archenholtz (traduite de l'allemande), Paris, 1804.

History of the Buccaneers of America, by James Burney, F.R.S., London, 1816.

L'Amiral du Casse (1646–1715), par le Baron Robert du Casse, Paris, 1876.

A Study of Attacks upon Fortified Harbors, by Lieut. Commander W. L. Rodgers, U.S.N. (Proc. U.S. Naval Inst., vol. xxx, no. 3).

VERNON

Printed Sources

History of Jamaica in Thirteen Letters from a Gentleman to his Friend, London, 1740.

An Account of the Expedition to Cartagena, with Explanatory Notes and Observations, by Sir Charles Knowles, London, 1743.

A Journal of the Expedition to Cartagena, with notes, in Answer to a late Pamphlet, Entitled an Account of the Expedition to Carthagena, London, 1744.

Authentic Papers Relating to the Expedition Against Cartagena containing Original Letters between the Admiral and the General, their Councils of War, etc., London, 1744.

Original Papers Relating to the Expedition to Cartagena, London, 1744.

Memorial of Admiral Vernon from Contemporary Authorities, by William Frederick Vernon, privately printed, London, 1861.

A Study of Attacks upon Fortified Harbors, by Lieut.-Commander W. L. Rodgers, U.S.N. (Proc. U.S. Naval Inst., vol. xxx, no. 3).

Massachusetts in the Expedition under Admiral Vernon, by W. K. Watkins (Year Book, Soc. of Colonial Wars, Boston, 1899).

Admiral Vernon and the Navy; a Memoir, by Douglas Ford, London, 1907.

Manuscripts

Letters and Reports of Blas de Leso, General Commanding the Spanish Galleons at Cartagena.

Letters and Reports of the President of Panamá, Dionesio Martinez de la Vega, particularly a long report to the King of Spain, dated at Panamá, 12 Feb., 1740 (N.S.).

Copy of a Diary of a resident of Cartagena during invasion by Admiral Vernon, 1741. (Original at University of Colombia, Bogotá.)

Correspondence between Admiral Vernon and Governor Trelawney of Jamaica in connection with the trial of Sir Chaloner Ogle for assault before the Chief Justice of Jamaica in 1742.

Letters between the Vice King of Santa Fé, Governor of Cartagena, and Admiral Vernon.

Letters of Vernon, Wentworth, and others contained in the large and valuable collection called the "Vernon-Wager Manuscripts," now in the Library of Congress, Washington.

Various documents, letters, and notes in the Public Archives and private collections at Cartagena, Colombia.

RODNEY

Printed Sources

Letters from Sir George Bridges now Lord Rodney to His Majesty's Ministers, etc., privately printed, 1781.

The Life and Correspondence of the late Admiral Lord Rodney, by Major-General Mundy, London, 1830. (Containing letters to and from Rodney and Lady Rodney, the Earl of Sandwich, Philip Stevens, the Admiralty Secretary, Sir Samuel Hood, the Earl of Carlisle, the Comte de Grasse, Wm. Pitt, various British and foreign officers and others.)

The Operations of the French Fleet under the Count de Grasse in 1781–2, as described in two contemporary journals, privately printed for the Bradford Club, New York, 1864.

Rodney's Victory over De Grasse, by Commander Nankivell, R.N., in the Journal of the Institute of Jamaica, vol. 11, no. 2, Kingston, 1895.

The contemporaneous issues of the *London Magazine* and other publications, containing official orders, dispatches, and reports.

Manuscripts

Various unpublished reports, letters, maps and naval diagrams in private collections and public archives.

INDEX

INDEX

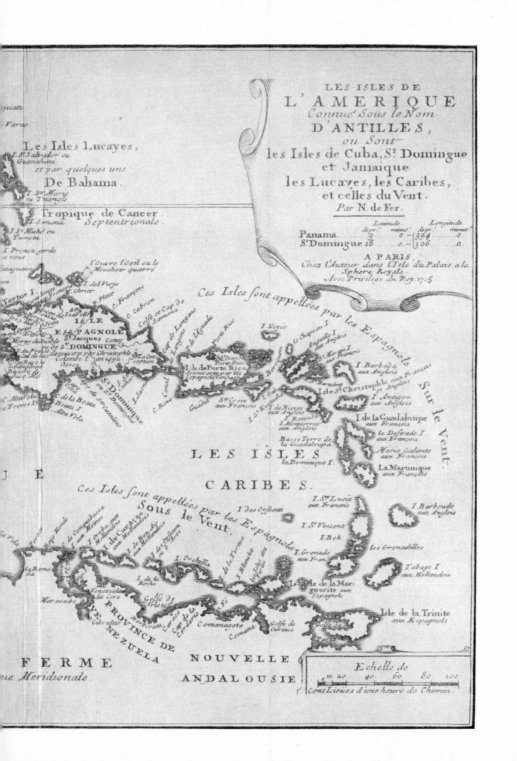